D1197564

J.R.R.
TOLKIEN:
THE MAKING OF A LEGEND

"J.R.R. Tolkien created a new form of literary legend with his histories of Middle-earth and, as result, has himself been accorded legendary status. Colin Duriez, who is well versed in the ways of Hobbits and other denizens of Tolkien's world, presents an engaging, intimate account of the author's life and work and the phenomenon that both have become. At a time when writings about *Tolkien* far outnumber writings by *him*, it is good to be able to commend such a well-researched and highly readable biography that captures the essence of the man and enables us to better understand and appreciate his extraordinary achievement."

Brian Sibley
Author of *The Hobbit: An Unexpected Journey Official Movie Guide*

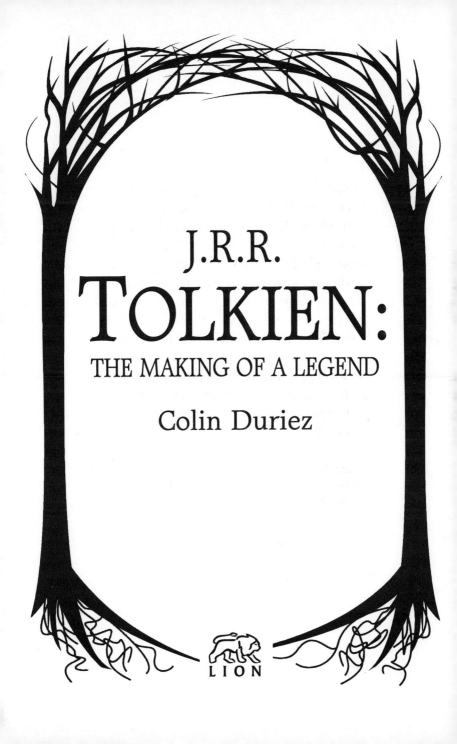

J.R.R. TOLKIEN:

THE MAKING OF A LEGEND

Colin Duriez

LION

Copyright © 2012 Colin Duriez

This edition copyright © 2012 Lion Hudson

The right of Colin Duriez to be identified
as the author of this work has been
asserted by him in accordance with the
Copyright, Designs and Patents Act 1988.

All rights reserved. No part of this
publication may be reproduced or
transmitted in any form or by any means,
electronic or mechanical, including
photocopy, recording, or any information
storage and retrieval system, without
permission in writing from the publisher.

Published by Lion Books
an imprint of
Lion Hudson plc
Wilkinson House, Jordan Hill Road,
Oxford OX2 8DR, England
www.lionhudson.com/lion

ISBN 978 0 7459 5514 8
e-ISBN 978 0 7459 5709 8

First edition 2012

Acknowledgments

Excerpts from *Tolkien and C.S. Lewis: The Gift
of Friendship*, Copyright © 2003 by Colin
Duriez, Paulist Press, Inc., New York/
Mahwah, N.J. Used with permission of
Paulist Press. www.paulistpress.com
pp. 14, 104, 199: *Now Read On* radio
interview with J.R.R. Tolkien reprinted by
permission of BBC Radio 4.
pp. 19–20, 21, 38–39, 41, 42, 45, 51, 66,
78, 78–79, 80, 94, 115, 128, 130, 134–35,
138, 139, 158, 167–68, 189: From *J.R.R.
Tolkien: A Biography* copyright © 1977
by Humphrey Carpenter. Reprinted by
permission of HarperCollins Publishers Ltd.
pp. 25–26, 29–30, 46, 52, 53, 81, 109,
118, 191, 198, 201: From *The Letters of
J.R.R. Tolkien* copyright © 2006 edited
by Humphrey Carpenter. Reprinted by
permission of HarperCollins Publishers Ltd.
p. 44: From *J.R.R. Tolkien: Author of the
Century* copyright © 2001 by Tom Shipy.
Reprinted by permission of HarperCollins
Publishers Ltd.
pp. 31, 58, 60, 143: The *Times* obituary
of J.R.R. Tolkien written by C.S. Lewis
reprinted by permission of The Times/
NI Syndication.
pp. 83–84: From *J.R.R. Tolkien Encyclopedia*

copyright © 2007 by Michael D.C. Drout.
Reprinted by permission of Routledge/
Copyright Clearance Center.
pp. 83, 89, 91, 95, 105: From *Tolkien
and the Great War* copyright © 2005 by
John Garth. Reprinted by permission of
HarperCollins Publishers Ltd.
pp. 115, 116: From *The Ring of Words:
Tolkien and the Oxford English Dictionary*
copyright © 2006 by Peter Gilliver, Jeremy
Marshall and Edmund Weiner. Reprinted
by permission of Oxford University Press.
p. 135: From *The Tolkien Relation* copyright
© 1968 by William Ready.
p. 136: From *Memoirs* copyright © 1992 by
Kingsley Amis. Reprinted by permission
of The Random House Group Limited and
The Wylie Agency.
p. 147: From *The Inklings: C.S. Lewis,
J.R.R. Tolkien, Charles Williams and their
friends* copyright © 1979 by Humphrey
Carpenter. Reprinted by permission of
HarperCollins Publishers Ltd and
C.S. Lewis Pte Ltd.
p. 150: Extracts by C.S. Lewis © copyright
C.S. Lewis Pte Ltd.
p. 166: From *C.S. Lewis: Memories and
Reflections* copyright © 1998 by John
Lawlor. Reprinted by permission of Spence
Publishing Company.
p. 202: From *Proceedings of the J.R.R. Tolkien
Centenary Conference 1992* copyright ©
1995 edited by Glen H. GoodKnight
and Patricia Reynolds. Reprinted by
permission of Mythopoeic Society.
p. 184: From *Arthurian Torso* copyright
© 1948 by C.S. Lewis. Reprinted by
permission of The C.S. Lewis Company Ltd.
p. 204: Review of *The Return of the King*
in the *New York Times* copyright © 1956 by
W.H. Auden. Reprinted by permission of
Curtis Brown, Ltd.
p. 203: From *Brothers and Friends: The Diaries
of Major Warren Hamilton* copyright © 1988
by Clyde S. Kilby and Marjorie Lamp.
Reprinted by permission of HarperCollins
Publishers Ltd.

Cover photo © Pamela Chandler/
ArenaPAL/TopFoto

A catalogue record for this book is
available from the British Library

Printed and bound in Great Britain,
September 2012, LH06

Contents

FOREWORD   7

1. "I AM IN FACT A HOBBIT…"   11

2. EDITH   24

3. SCHOOLDAYS AND THE T.C.B.S.   38

4. OXFORD AND THE DAWN OF A NEW LIFE   55

5. THE SHADOW OF WAR   73

6. WAR AND LOSS   86

7. RECOVERY, "W", AND HALF A MILLION
   WORDS   103

8. LEEDS AND DRAGONS   121

9. OXFORD AND C.S. LEWIS   131

10. OF HOBBITS AND INKLINGS   155

11. TOLKIEN'S SECOND WAR   177

12. THE STRUGGLE TO PUBLISH   192

13. THE TOLKIEN PHENOMENON, AND
    FAREWELL   213

AFTERWORD   220

NOTES   221

SELECT BIBLIOGRAPHY   233

INDEX   236

To
Abigail Perriss,
Max Hopson Ferris
and
Poppy Webb

Foreword

There it was in the bookshop. A book called *The Hobbit* with a cover picture of a dragon soaring, an arrow embedded in his breast. I picked it up and opened it – the runes and end paper maps were intriguing. Quickly I bought the book and was soon following Bilbo's adventures as he made his way towards the Lonely Mountain. The author's name I recognized as a close friend of C.S. Lewis, an author I had recently discovered. I was reading his autobiography, *Surprised By Joy*, at the time.

The next time I visited the library, I looked under "T". The three red cloth-bound volumes stood out. In great excitement I opened them. *The Fellowship of the Ring* had much more about Hobbits. I borrowed it, the first of the three volumes of *The Lord of the Rings*, and began another stage of discovery.

Today, it is difficult to imagine a world without J.R.R. Tolkien's stories of Middle-earth and Elves, Wizards, and Hobbits. His is a household name from Tunbridge Wells to Toronto, Kyoto to Cape Town. Long before the successful movies, the books of *The Hobbit* and *The Lord of the Rings* had a global popularity. Their devoted readers included plumbers and postgraduate students, IT specialists and rich merchant bankers, car mechanics and teachers, pensioners and children. The Tolkien phenomenon began within the cultural upheavals of the sixties and created an unprecedented demand for fantasy and otherworldly stories like the Harry Potter series, the Twilight series, and others that fill large sections of bookstores around the planet.

Who was the man who became a legend? Where did the stories and underlying mythology of Middle-earth come from? This is the story of an intensely private, brilliant, and eccentric professor in a specialist university discipline whose imagination was in touch with our basic hunger for stories that, like all stories that have stood out and survived over the ages, nourish the spirit. When he sought to get *The Lord of the Rings* – the fruit of a dozen or so years of writing – into print, he had difficulty in settling on a publisher. When he did, his publisher, though enthusiastic, treated the work as a loss-making venture, little realizing the wealth it would create both for the company and its author. Tolkien's own life was hit hard as an orphan suffering financial hardship. His guardian for three years forbad him to even communicate with the woman with whom he had fallen in love. After his brilliance was eventually recognized at Oxford, he was traumatized by his service in the Battle of the Somme in the First World War.

That is only part of the story of J.R.R. Tolkien. Behind the depths and richness of *The Lord of the Rings* is over fifty years of creation accompanying the languages, history, peoples, and geography of Middle-earth, with a consistent mythology and body of legends inspired by a formidable knowledge of early northwest European history and culture. Tolkien only became a legend by making a legend that has gripped the imagination of an astonishing variety of people throughout the world.

There are a couple of technical necessities I need to point out. One is that I have kept to Tolkien's own pluralization of "Dwarf" as "Dwarves" when referring to such characters in his stories. As has become the custom when writing about Tolkien, the second is the necessity of distinguishing *The Silmarillion* published in 1977 (four years after Tolkien's death) from the vast number of unfinished drafts of stories, annals, lexicons, and accounts of the development of Elvish languages that Tolkien left upon his death. This vast repository is indicated as "The Silmarillion", because it was drafted as a particular part of the imagined history of Middle-earth that concerned the precious gems called the Silmarils, or relates to that period as its past or its future. *The Silmarillion* of 1977 is a concise and authoritative version drawn from the extant material, and edited by Tolkien's son, Christopher Tolkien.

I must acknowledge at least some of my debts to others in writing this biography. Over the years I have witnessed an astonishing outpouring of high-quality scholarship on J.R.R. Tolkien, some of which has been particularly helpful in creating a biography. The late Humphrey Carpenter's official biography of 1977 is still indispensible, even now that so many more of Tolkien's writings are available, not least because of his access to private documents and his ability to make sense of a universe of unfinished writings, diaries in code, and contradictory opinions. To him I must at least add the names of John Garth, Wayne G. Hammond and Christina Scull, Brian Sibley, Bob Blackham, Douglas A. Anderson, Matthew Dickerson, Michael Drout, Tom Shippey, Colin Manlove, Dimitra Fimi, Verlyn Fliegar, Corey Olsen, John Rateliff, Walter Hooper, the late Clyde S. Kilby, and A.N. Wilson. While many of their works are not biographical, these have provided insights, hard facts, and inspiration. Though my book is not intended for scholars but for ordinary readers wishing to explore the life of Tolkien and how it relates to his stories of Middle-earth, the wisdom from those

I've mentioned, and many others, is a necessary background. My thanks are also due to The Marion E. Wade Center, Wheaton College, Illinois, and the Bodleian Library, Oxford, with its J.R.R. Tolkien special collection, for their unique resources. Thanks to Paulist Press for allowing me to adapt some material from my book, *Tolkien and C.S. Lewis: The Gift of Friendship*. I must also thank my indefatigable and encouraging editor and friend, Alison Hull, Kirsten Etheridge, Jessica Tinker, Margaret Milton, Leisa Nugent, and other helpful staff at Lion Hudson. Thanks also to my wife, Cindy Zudys, not only for the support of encouragement, but also for her hard work in keeping money coming in during tough times. My final debt is to fans large and small, some no doubt with hairy feet and perhaps pointed ears, whom I've met from many countries. Their love of Tolkien's work is infectious, and their knowledge often terrifying, especially when it comes to questions at the end of a talk. I'm immensely glad that when I gave my very first talk to The Tolkien Society, and the serious questions were winding down, my reply to the query "Do Balrogs have wings?" was "I don't know". If I had said yes or no, the debate would still be going on, and I expect I wouldn't have had time to write books.

Colin Duriez,
Keswick, Cumbria, April 2012

1

"I am in fact a Hobbit..."

There was turmoil in the Tolkien household. Baby Ronald
had disappeared. It was usual for the infant to be resting in
the cool of the house throughout the middle hours of the day.
There were grounds for many fears, not least of prowling
beasts such as jackals or wolves who might wander into the
town from the dust of the desolate expanse of grassland that
opened nearby beyond the houses.

The Tolkiens treated their two black servants, a maid and
a young man called Izaak, fairly. Mabel Tolkien disliked many
settlers' attitudes to the natives in the Orange Free State,
and though considerably upset, seems to have accepted
Izaak's simple explanation that he had carried off Ronald
to his village to proudly demonstrate a white baby. Later,
when he had his own son, Izaak named him, in appreciation
of the Tolkiens, "Izaak Mr Tolkien Victor" – "Victor" added to
honour Queen Victoria.

John Ronald Reuel Tolkien, to give the infant his full name,[1]
had been born on 3 January 1892 in Bloemfontein, southern
Africa, the first son of English citizens Arthur Reuel and
Mabel Tolkien. The parents were from Birmingham, in the

Midlands, and Mabel Suffield, as she then was, had sailed to Cape Town to marry Arthur, a banker who had preceded her to Africa to seek better prospects in the mineral-rich country. The Bank of Africa had promoted him to be their manager in Bloemfontein, at the heart of the Orange Free State, around 700 miles from Cape Town; discoveries of gold and diamonds had expanded the banking business there. Mabel Suffield left England in March 1891. The wedding ceremony took place the following month in Cape Town Anglican Cathedral.

In Bloemfontein the family lived "over the bank in Maitland Street: beyond were the dusty, treeless plains of the veldt". Mabel described her firstborn in a letter home to her mother-in-law: "Baby does look such a fairy when he's *very* much dressed-up in white frills and white shoes. When he's very much *un*dressed I think he looks more of an elf still." That baby would grow to become a brilliant scholar and storyteller who, decades later, reintroduced marvellous and formidable Elves of European folklore and legend to new generations of rapt readers. They were far from the saccharine, dainty fairies of his Victorian childhood. However, Mabel never was to know of her son's global celebrity.

The scare over baby Ronald's disappearance was only one of Mabel's worries about her infant, whom she saw as delicate. There was an occasion, of which Ronald carried dim memories in later life, when as a toddler he ran through long, dry grass in their large garden and disturbed a tarantula spider (they can be the size of a man's hand), which bit its venom into him. Crying, he ran into the house, where his nurse calmly sucked out the poison. Ronald remembered running and crying, but nothing of the huge spider. It may however have been the seed of many references to giant spiders in his stories, not least Ungoliant, the ancient creature who gobbled up the light of the world in the earliest age of Middle-earth, and of course her descendant Shelob, whom the Hobbits Frodo and Sam encountered on their perilous way into the dark land of Mordor, the realm of the Dark Lord, Sauron.

Even deeper than these dangers to Ronald, however, was the worry of the child's health in the oppressive heat of much of the year, and from the dust swept from the windy veldt. As Mabel's concern deepened, she became increasingly anxious about Arthur's lack of interest in returning to England at some stage. To her it was obvious that he was reluctant even to have a break in England, though leave was due to him. Unlike Mabel, Arthur was in his element in Africa as he faced the tough challenges of building his bank's client base in the harsh environment of the Boer heartland, with its general antipathy to the British. His wife felt fear when she read what Arthur had written to his father in Birmingham one day: "I think I shall do well in this country and do not think I should settle down well in England again for a permanency." Then Mabel found herself also having to put off thoughts of a visit home: she was pregnant with their second son, Hilary, born 17 February 1894.

Hilary turned out to be sturdier than his older brother, who became increasingly sickly in that harsh climate. It became evident to the couple that the relentless heat was damaging Ronald's health. Mabel was desperate. In November of 1894, she took baby Hilary and Ronald to the cooler air of the coast, hundreds of miles away near Cape Town. Years later Ronald could summon up dim memories of the endless train journey and a broad sandy shore. In a BBC radio interview he once said: "I can remember bathing in the Indian Ocean when I was not quite two."[2] Upon the return of Mabel and the children to Bloemfontein later that month, Arthur made arrangements for their journey to England. He would follow later, he said. Ronald's last memory of his father was a vivid image of him painting "A.R. Tolkien" on their cabin trunk as Mabel and the boys prepared to leave – a trunk Ronald kept and treasured in later years. In one unfinished story written almost half a century later, "The Notion Club Papers", he gave himself the fictional name of "John Arthurson".

While Arthur remained, absorbed in his work responsibilities, Mabel and the children sailed for England at the beginning of April 1895. The three, at first, stayed with Mabel's parents and one of her sisters, Jane, in their small family house in Ashfield Road, King's Heath, Birmingham. Ronald was confused by the change and sometimes expected to see the verandah of his home in Bloemfontein protruding from the Suffield home. Many years later he recalled: "I can still remember going down the road in Birmingham and wondering what had happened to the big gallery, what happened to the balcony." Also novel and strange was seeing for the first time a real Christmas tree after the "barren, arid heat".

During this visit, when the three were about to return to southern Africa, Arthur was taken ill with rheumatic fever and then unexpectedly died after severe haemorrhaging. He was only thirty-nine. A few days after his death on 15 February 1896, he was buried in the Anglican graveyard in Bloemfontein. His passing closed the chapter of the Tolkiens' life in southern Africa. It meant however that they were not caught up in the upheaval of the Boer War that happened relatively soon after (1899–1902).

Mabel was now a single parent, with very limited means. Soon the three moved to Sarehole, in the more healthy countryside. Their new home, 5 Gracewell, was a smart and good-sized semi-detached cottage almost opposite the pond side of Sarehole Mill, then about a mile south of the city of Birmingham. Though so near to the metropolis, they were, in fact, in the very heart of rural Worcestershire. With only horses and carts, it was "long ago in the quiet of the world, when there was less noise and more green" (to use words from Tolkien's *The Hobbit* describing the Shire in Middle-earth). Mabel, a highly talented and resourceful woman, educated her boys until they entered formal schooling. Among other things, Mabel taught Ronald to read, and later introduced him to calligraphy, drawing, Latin, French, piano (unsuccessfully), and botany.

The quiet Worcestershire village (which later became part of Warwickshire through boundary changes) was soon, for Ronald, his heart-home, associated with memories of the mother he was so soon to lose: "the Shire is very like the kind of world in which I first became aware of things…. If your first Christmas tree is a wilting eucalyptus and if you're normally troubled by heat and sand – then… just at the age when imagination is opening out, suddenly [to] find yourself in a quiet Warwickshire village, I think it engenders a particular love of what you might call central Midlands English countryside, based on good water stones and elm trees and small quiet rivers and so on, and of course rustic people about."[3] The "rustic" local children derided the Tolkien boy's long hair (the custom for middle-class little boys).

Sarehole Mill made a particular impression on Ronald's imagination: "There was an old mill that really did grind corn with two millers, a great big pond with swans on it, a sandpit, a wonderful dell with flowers, a few old-fashioned village houses and, further away, a stream with another mill."[4] Sarehole Mill was an old brick mill with a tall chimney. Though it was powered by a steam engine, a stream still ran under its great wheel. The mill, with its frightening miller's son, made a deep impression on Ronald's and also Hilary's imaginations.

Ronald and his younger brother nicknamed the terrifying miller's son "the White Ogre". Hilary remembered a farmer, nicknamed "the Black Ogre", who terrorized the local children. (He once chased Ronald for picking mushrooms.) In a letter much later Tolkien speaks of the old miller and his son bringing terror and wonder to him as a little child. In another letter he wrote of living his early years "in 'the Shire' in a pre-mechanical age". He added that he was a Hobbit in fact, though not in size. Like Hobbits he relished gardens, trees, and farmlands that were not mechanized. He too smoked a pipe and liked his food plain. In the drab mid twentieth century when the popularity of his stories exploded, he dared to wear ornamental waistcoats. He was fond of mushrooms fresh from the field and liked expressing his very basic sense of humour, which some found tiresome. He also recorded that as an adult, he went to bed late and, if he could, got up late. Like Hobbits, he travelled little. In *The Lord of the Rings* he wrote of a mill in Hobbiton, located on the Water, which was torn down and replaced by a brick building that polluted both the air and water. There is a resemblance between the view up the rural lane in which the family lived in Sarehole, with the Mill to the right, and a detailed illustration Tolkien made of Hobbiton for *The Hobbit,* the forerunner to his *The Lord of the Rings.*

Sarehole Mill survived the brick tsunami of Birmingham's urban spread and is now preserved as a visitor's centre. Visitors are able to catch a glimpse of Tolkien's childhood world and an important historical monument of the industrial revolution that changed the world. The large, deep pond that Ronald and Hilary knew so well is there, and the mill buildings, with their large chimney, are still recognizable from those lost days. Nearby, in recognition of Tolkien, is the Shire Country Park, and Moseley Bog, possibly inspiration for the Old Forest on the edge of the Shire in *The Lord of the Rings*.

It may have been around this time in Sarehole when another important feature of Ronald's teeming imagination was born: his recurring dream of a great flood, a green wave surging across the lands. Eventually, after a long gestation, this part of his memory was incorporated into the same imagined world in which the Shire was a part – Middle-earth. The dream became Tolkien's fictional account of the destruction of Númenor, his own version of the ancient story of the drowned land of Atlantis.

In 1900, five years after leaving Africa, Ronald entered King Edward's School, Birmingham's top grammar school, then located near New Street Station, in the city centre. His fees were paid by an uncle. Its buildings (now demolished) bore the mark of its architect, Sir Charles Barry, who also designed the current Houses of Parliament in London. At this time Mabel Tolkien, along with her sister May, was received into the Roman Catholic Church, despite painful opposition from her Unitarian father and Tolkien in-laws, who were Baptist. They cut off financial support to the single mother, resulting in a deepening poverty. Mother and sons moved from their rural setting to just inside the city, to Moseley, to be somewhat nearer to the Birmingham Oratory in Edgbaston. Founded by Cardinal Newman in the 1850s, this had become Mabel's spiritual home after trying other more local Roman Catholic churches. The visionary John Henry Newman (1801–90) had done much to revitalize Roman Catholicism, bringing his Oxford learning, imagination, and independence into the life of that Church. Moseley was on the tram route to the city centre, making it easier for Ronald to commute to school.

The next year they had to move again, to a nearby terrace close by King's Heath station. Behind their new home was a railway embankment, full of wild flowers and grasses (another love of Ronald's). By now he was about nine years of age, and his brother, Hilary, around seven. They were becoming used to the squeal of coal wagons being shunted in the coal yard a short way up the railway tracks. Trains came from the mining valleys of South Wales over a hundred miles away, dragging coal wagons for Birmingham's thriving industries. Ronald noticed the names on the sides of the wagons: Welsh places like *Blaen-Rhondda, Maerdy, Nantyglo,* and *Tredegar*.

In the BBC interview in 1971, mentioned earlier, Tolkien revealed something of the significance of this encounter with Welsh place names. In many ways, this boyhood experience marks the early seeds of the tales of his invented world of Middle-earth, a world of Hobbits, Elves, and darker beings like goblins and dragons. In that interview Tolkien explained his fascination: "Welsh has always attracted me by its style and sound more than any other; even though I first only saw it on coal trucks, I always wanted to know what it was about." He went on to say that his stories almost always began with a name. "Give me a name and it produces a story, not the other way about normally." He says that of modern languages, Welsh, and later Finnish, had been the greatest inspiration for his writing, including the creation of *The Lord of the Rings*. Welsh, in fact, was to inspire one of the two main branches of the languages of Elves that he created and, as a result, many of the names in his invented world of Middle-earth, such as *Arwen* the Elven Queen, the River *Anduin*, the *Rohirrim* people and *Gwaihir* the giant eagle.

Later the Tolkien family moved to a plain house in Oliver Road, which was almost a slum (now demolished as part of inner-city improvements). It was in the generally prosperous Edgbaston district, a short walk from the Birmingham Oratory and close by a spacious reservoir. For a time the Tolkien brothers were taken out of King Edward's School by Mabel and enrolled at the Oratory's own school, St Philip's, where fees were much lower. In 1903 however Ronald gained a scholarship for King Edward's, just two miles away from his Edgbaston home, and resumed study there in the autumn. Ronald took his first communion at Christmas that year, marking his fervent devotion to his mother's Roman Catholic faith.

During the Christmas holidays that year, Mabel wrote to her mother-in-law, Mary Jane Tolkien, enclosing some drawings by Ronald and Hilary:

> You said you like one of the boys' drawings better than anything bought with their money so they've done these for you. Ronald has really done his [drawing] splendidly this year – he has just been having quite an exhibition in Father Francis' room – he has worked hard since he

broke up [from school] on December 16th, and so have
I to find fresh subjects: – I haven't been out for almost
a *month* – not even to The Oratory! – but the nasty wet
muggy weather is making me better and since Ronald
broke up I have been able to rest in the mornings. I keep
having whole *weeks* of utter sleeplessness, which added
to the internal cold and sickness have made it almost
impossible to go on.

I found a postal order for 2/6 which you sent the
boys some time ago – a year at least – which has been
mislaid. They've been in town all afternoon spending
this and a little bit more on things they wanted to give.
– They've done all my Xmas shopping – Ronald can
match silk lining or any art shade like a true "Parisian
Modiste". Is it his Artist or Draper ancestry coming out?
– He is going along at a great rate at school – he knows
far more Greek than I do Latin – he says he is going to
do German with me these holidays – though at present I
feel more like Bed.

One of the clergy, a young, merry one, is teaching
Ronald to play chess – he says he has read *too* much,
everything fit for a boy under fifteen, and he doesn't
know any single classical thing to recommend him.[5]

Through their contact with St Philip's School Mabel and her
sons had met Father Francis Xavier Morgan, who was steeped
in Cardinal Newman's ideals of education. Francis Morgan
was a parish priest attached to the Oratory, and he had served
under Newman. Father Francis provided friendship, counsel,
and money for the fatherless family. With the boys often ill and
the mother developing diabetes, he enabled them to lodge in a

pretty Oratory cottage in 1904. Woodside Cottage[6] was close by the Oratory's rural retreat in nearby Rednal village, deep in the Worcestershire countryside and on the Lickey Hills. The rural atmosphere there was like that of Sarehole and delighted the three. Despite the setting, Mabel continued to decline, forcing Father Francis to seek some respite for her from caring for her sons. Ronald spent the summer term in Hove, on the south coast, with his aunt Jane Neave and her husband Edwin, while Hilary stayed with his Suffield grandparents.

After the boys returned, Mabel reported to her mother-in-law: "Boys look *ridiculously well* compared to the weak white ghosts that met me on train 4 weeks ago!!! Hilary has got tweed suit and his first Etons today! and looks *immense*. – We've had perfect weather. Boys will write first wet day but what with Bilberry-gathering – Tea in Hay – Kite-flying with Fr Francis – sketching – Tree Climbing – they've never enjoyed a holiday so much."[7]

While Mabel continued to be confined, Ronald, when school was back after the summer holiday, would catch a train to school, walking more than a mile to the station. He started off early, and returned late, with Hilary sometimes meeting him with a lamp. Mabel died in Woodside Cottage some months later, on 14 November 1904, succumbing to her diabetes, which in those days was untreatable. She was buried in the churchyard of St Peter's Roman Catholic Church, Bromsgrove, with her grave marked with a cross similar to those on the graves of the Oratory fathers. The sight of the two young orphans standing beside her grave must have rended the hearts of mourners. Ronald remembered, years later: "I witnessed (half-comprehending) the heroic sufferings and early death in extreme poverty of my mother who brought me into the Church; and received the astonishing charity of Francis Morgan. But I fell in love with the Blessed Sacrament from the beginning..."

Ronald remembered his mother as a woman of great gifts, beauty, and wit. She was deeply acquainted, he perceived, with suffering and grief. He believed implicitly that her early death, at thirty-four, was precipitated by what he called the "persecution" of her Roman Catholic faith by the Nonconformist relatives. The impact of her death on the brothers on top of the earlier loss of their father can only be imagined. Tolkien wrote far later in life, "It is to my mother, who taught me (until I obtained a scholarship) that I owe my tastes for philology, especially of Germanic languages, and for romance." By "romance" Tolkien meant stories and poetry that gave a glimpse of other worlds, and which made a direct appeal to the imagination in their strangeness and wonder. "Philology" was his chosen area of knowledge and scholarship, which he was later to teach at Oxford and write learnedly about. It is a study that takes into account the history of both a language and its literature, rather than focusing only upon one or the other. Tolkien became a giant in this field, like Jacob Grimm before him, famous with his brother Wilhelm for his collection of folk and fairy stories.

From his youth Ronald Tolkien thought much about his mother and father; the loss of them deeply affected his sense of identity in differing ways. They had been born Arthur Tolkien and Mabel Suffield. Ronald saw a contrast between the Tolkiens and the Suffields, and identified himself largely with the latter family. The Tolkiens several generations before his birth had been German immigrants, and the name gave rise to family myths of its origin, as is common in such situations. One story that appealed to Ronald was that the name derived from a nickname given to an ancestor: *tollkühn*, "foolhardy". (Tolkien later gave himself another fictional name of "Professor Rashbold" in his unfinished "The Notion Club Papers".) The recent generations were piano makers who had fallen on hard times. The Suffields, in contrast, he felt were thoroughly English, rooted in the Evesham area of Worcestershire. As West Midlanders they belonged to a region Tolkien grew to love for its dialects and geography. His mother, Mabel, represented for him all that was best in the Suffields. He wrote, "Though a Tolkien by name, I am a Suffield by tastes, talents and upbringing." Worcestershire (symbolized in Sarehole) was, for him, home: "Any corner of that county (however fair or squalid) is in an indefinable way 'home' to me, as no other part of the world is." The sense of difference between his Tolkien and Suffield heritage was heightened by his mother's conversion to Roman Catholicism. The Tolkiens were Nonconformists (as were the Suffields), but his mother's new faith, it seems likely, was to her son quintessentially English and West Midlands, and rooted in the long medieval period. His own Roman Catholic convictions were emotionally tied strongly to his mother throughout his life.

2

Edith

The death of Mabel Tolkien magnified the uncertainty that had dominated the lives of Ronald and Hilary. Ronald was twelve years old, and his brother only ten. Ronald had lost the entire summer term at school while he stayed with his Aunt Jane and her new husband Edwin Neave in far-off Hove. During that autumn term he had each school day faced his long commute by foot and train to the city centre from Woodside Cottage. It was no surprise that in his school examinations in December, Ronald came eleventh out of fifteen in his class. With their mother gone, the boys could no longer stay at the cottage.

Mabel had formally willed that their guardian was to be Father Francis Morgan. It was clear that she wished her sons to remain under the care of the Roman Catholic Church. The story would have been different if either the Tolkien or Suffield relations had taken on their guardianship; the boys would then have faced either a Baptist or Unitarian upbringing.

Father Francis gamely took on the burden with his usual enthusiasm. He faced an immediate dilemma. The Oratory in Edgbaston could not house the two orphans. Boys from the Oratory Public School used part of the building as dormitories, taking up almost all available space. As a temporary expedient, the boys stayed with their uncle Lawrence Tolkien in King's Norton, then a village outside of the city boundaries, but on a main railway line into the centre. This made easy travelling to King Edward's School.

A solution came to Father Francis that seemed satisfactory in several ways. Mabel's younger brother, Will, who had died earlier that year, had left a childless widow, the boys' Auntie Bea (Beatrice Suffield, née Barlett). She was willing to take them as lodgers, and had no strong religious views. She had little money and was glad to receive the £4 and 16 shillings from Father Francis each month. Auntie Bea lived at 25 Stirling Road. It was a side street off the main road through Edgbaston. The boys shared the top-floor bedroom in her gloomy house, which had an expansive view of myriads of rooftops, with factory chimneys in the distance. There was a tantalizing glimpse of distant countryside.

It was some years before their guardian realized how unhappy Ronald and Hilary were at their aunt's. She did little more than provide board and lodgings, and she lacked affection towards them. Her recent widowing may have been a factor in this. Her absence of empathy was evident when, one day, Ronald came across the ashes of his mother's letters and papers. His Auntie Bea seemed to have no idea they might be important to him when she burned them.

The Oratory was close to Stirling Road. Its founder, Cardinal Newman, might have considered it in keeping with the ethos he created that the Oratory became something of a home to the boys. Years later, an elderly Ronald wrote to his son Michael: "I had the advantage of a (then) first rate school and that of a 'good Catholic home' – 'in excelsis': virtually a junior inmate of the Oratory house, which contained many learned fathers.... Observance of religion was strict. Hilary and I were supposed to, and usually did, serve Mass before getting on our bikes to go to school in New Street...."[1] Ronald and Hilary would eat breakfast in the Fathers' refectory after serving Mass for Father Francis. They liked to spin the compliant kitchen cat around in the revolving food hatch or "drum" (which linked the kitchen and the refectory) before leaving for school.

Hilary had joined Ronald as a pupil at King Edward's School after gaining a scholarship. Sometimes they cycled to school or took a horse-drawn tram, and sometimes walked, or combined walking and catching a tram if running late. Their route took them down the broad, tree-lined Hagley Road to the extensive intersection called Five Ways, then along Broad Street toward the city centre and past the city hall, after which King Edward's large and grimy Gothic school building soon rose above New Street.

Ronald and Hilary soon became even more familiar with their Edgbaston neighbourhood. The Oratory's community featured large for them, as a place of security and worship, and with their daily attendance there before school. There is no doubt that Ronald would have taken in its architecture, and the ornaments of its chapel. He, like many children, would have been fascinated by the construction of a basilica-style church to replace the temporary chapel. The new church had been the vision of Cardinal Newman, though its construction did not begin until years after his death. The foundations were started in 1903, and Ronald and Hilary, the following year, would have seen its outer structure being built around the existing chapel in which they worshipped. The nave was finished by 1906, and the transept by 1909. The old chapel remained in use for the first three years of construction.

The boys participated enthusiastically in the Oratory's community outreach. According to the Parish Magazine (May 1909): "Three patrols of Scouts under the Brothers Tolkien, have been started, and they marched smartly in the wake of the Boys Brigade on Easter Monday. When they have done a little more drill, we shall ask some of our friends to help towards providing them with shirts, haversacks, etc."[2] As the Scout movement had only been started two years before by Robert Baden-Powell, the Tolkien brothers could be considered pioneers! The new movement aimed to support boys (and later, girls) in their physical, mental, and spiritual development, so that they were equipped to play constructive roles in society. Ronald may have had a copy of *Scouting for Boys,* the classic manual by Baden-Powell published the year before. Sam Gamgee the Hobbit displayed scouting skills when he cooked rabbit for Frodo and himself in *The Lord of the Rings.*

Outside of the Oratory, there was much to interest Ronald in Edgbaston. Next to Stirling Road was the self-explanatory Waterworks Road. It contained two landmarks, known locally as the "two towers", that dominated the skyline. One, with a blue and red brick neo-Gothic effect, formed the chimney of the local Victorian waterworks. The other is an eighteenth-century tower, slender and elegant, brutally named in the area "Perrott's Folly", after its maker. It was next to Humphrey Perrott's lodge, where there used to be an enclosed hunting park. There is much speculation that the twin towers might have been a seed of the Two Towers in Tolkien's *The Lord of the Rings.* Though an attractive idea, there is no certainty about this, not least as, to his publisher, Tolkien himself gave conflicting messages about what exactly the Two Towers in his story were.[3] During Ronald's childhood, however, there was a constant flurry of activity associated with the Waterworks Tower. It stood beside the engine room, boiler house, and workshops. Sometimes the immense chimney, like Saruman's workings around Orthanc (probably one of the "Two Towers" in volume two of *The Lord of the Rings*), would cough out black smoke, accompanied by the sound of pounding pumps, and these pumps' vibrations could be felt through the ground for a good distance around. The pumps supplied Birmingham and Aston with water from boreholes in the saturated rocks and sediments on which the city area is built.[4]

By the waterworks is a large reservoir that still feeds the city canal system. Rotton Park Reservoir, as it was named then, was a popular place for walking. Ronald and Hilary would have been able to amble around it. Indeed, according to historian Robert Blackham, the reservoir "in those days was like an inland seaside attraction. It had a bandstand, rowing boats for hire and beaches."[5] Today it is still the centre of many leisure activities.

Ronald had an insatiable intellectual curiosity, and there were no doubt many things in the Edgbaston area that engaged his interest. There is room for speculation. Did he, for instance, come across the name of Drogo of Edgbaston and later borrow it? In *The Lord of the Rings,* Drogo Baggins was the father of Frodo, and second cousin of Bilbo. According to the Domesday Book, soon after the Norman Conquest, Drogo of Whitley was a Lord in the hamlet of Edgbaston in AD 1086.[6] Many names in the West Midlands fit easily into Tolkien's linguistic world of the Shire. One name, of which Ronald clearly was aware, is that of Sam Gamgee (or rather, Dr Joseph Sampson Gamgee, to give him his full name). The widow of this famous surgeon lived over the road from Ronald's lodgings in Stirling Road. "Gamgee" was a household name in the area for what we call "cotton wool", the cotton dressing that was invented by Dr Gamgee. Gamgee was a friend of Joseph Lister[7] and also Louis Pasteur. Another name that seems to have registered with Ronald is that of a pub on the Hagley Road that Ronald and Hilary passed on their way to school. "The Ivy Bush" turns up as the name of a favourite tavern for Frodo, Sam, and their friends on the Bywater Road near Hobbiton, in *The Lord of the Rings*.[8]

As well as their involvement with the life of the Oratory, Ronald and Hilary had regular contact with their relatives, and visited them during school holidays. Ronald and Hilary, of course, had stayed with separate relatives during their mother's illness, and both had then stayed a short while with an uncle after her death. There were two aunts, one in Newcastle upon Tyne and one in nearby Moseley, sisters of their father. Then there was Mabel's elder sister, their Aunt May, who was married to a businessman called Walter Incledon. Their two daughters were Marjorie and Mary, with Marjorie a year older than Ronald, and Mary a year younger than Hilary. It was with the Incledons that the boys mostly stayed. They lived south of the metropolis in Barnt Green, deep in Worcestershire, not far from Rednal and the cottage in which Mabel and her sons had stayed until her death.

Late in life Tolkien recalled, in a letter to his son Michael, telling his cousin Marjorie about the impact of his mother's death: "... when I was not yet thirteen after the death of my mother… vainly waving a hand at the sky saying 'it is so empty and cold'." What he tried to tell Marjorie was his feeling "like a castaway left on a barren island under a heedless sky after the loss of a great ship".[9]

An indication of how close Ronald felt to his cousins Marjorie and Mary is that he was caught up in their invention of languages, something that was at the very core of his creativity. They helped him to realize that he was not alone in this desire; indeed, he became convinced, later in life, that this activity was not at all unusual in children. His own invention of languages was to lead to his creation of Middle-earth, where there was a setting and history for such languages. There were peoples who used them, such as Elves, orcs, Hobbits, and Ents.

When the children were younger, Marjorie and Mary used a simple language called "Animalic", so called because mostly animal names were substituted for words. Ronald happily participated in the game. Tolkien's official biographer, Humphrey Carpenter, gives the example sentence *Dog nightingale woodpecker forty,* which meant "You are an ass". Marjorie eventually grew tired of the very limited Animalic, whereupon Ronald and his cousin Mary worked upon a more advanced language that they called "Nevbosh" – that is, the "new nonsense". It was made up of disguised words from Latin, English, and French. For many years Ronald was to call his later invented languages such as Elvish, and early stories that correlated with them, his personal "nonsense" or "hobby", even though they behaved like real languages and histories would in a real geography.

In an interview late in his life, Tolkien revealed that he had "invented several languages" when he was "only about eight or nine", but that he had "destroyed them" as his mother "disapproved. She thought of my languages as a useless frivolity taking up time that could be better spent in studying."[10]

The constant attention of Father Francis, however, provided more continuity in the lives of Ronald and Hilary than visits to relations (and even, for many years, more security than their lives at King Edward's School, as important as that would become for Ronald). Their guardian kept a careful eye on them, according to his limited knowledge of children. Not only did he generously supplement the meagre income from a small investment Arthur Tolkien had left his wife at the time of his sudden, unexpected death, he also saw that they had board and lodgings, and spiritual and emotional support. As part of this he would take them off to the Lickey Hills. He would also carefully plan holidays for them. One favourite location helped to install (or more likely, restore) in Ronald a desire for the sea that stayed with him constantly throughout his life, and which is woven into his tales of Middle-earth. C.S. Lewis remembered: "Of Fr Morgan Tolkien always spoke with the warmest gratitude and affection."[11]

Each summer Father Francis would take the boys by train to one of his favourite resorts, Lyme Regis in West Dorset, on England's south coast. A branch line had opened to the resort only in 1903 because the terrain between the main line at Axminster and Lyme Regis made construction very difficult and expensive.

The trio would stay at the Three Cups hotel.[12] It was a brief, steep walk down Broad Street to the promenade, then a short distance west to Lyme Regis's harbour, crammed with fishing boats. Beside it the Cobb magnificently jutted out, snake-like. This features in Jane Austen's *Persuasion* and in John Fowles' 1969 novel, *The French Lieutenant's Woman*. Beyond the Cobb westward is the landmark Undercliff, a landslip that extends for miles. A particularly dramatic slip in the nineteenth century exposed a treasury of fossils. On one occasion Ronald found a prehistoric jawbone, and conjectured that it was from a dragon! The boy adored the coast scape of Lyme, exploring it on dry days and sketching it when wet. Some of his youthful but accomplished sketches are preserved in Oxford's Bodleian Library and include an image of the harbour.

The summer holidays in Lyme gave Father Francis many opportunities to talk with the boys. After several holidays this led to his discovery in 1907 that Ronald and Hilary were unhappy lodging with their Auntie Bea in Stirling Road. He resolved to find them more congenial lodgings.

Mrs Faulkner came to mind. Her husband was a wine merchant (Father Francis had a professional interest in wine from his family background). She was active in the Oratory parish and took in lodgers at her home at 37 Duchess Road, very near the Oratory. Mrs Faulkner's musical evenings were popular with some of the Oratory Fathers. The boys moved into their new lodgings at the beginning of 1908. So it was that Ronald met Edith Bratt, who not only helped with the musical evenings (she was a gifted pianist) but lodged on the floor below them. She was an orphan like they were. Edith was small, slender, and pretty, with grey eyes. She did not look three years older than Ronald. Though just sixteen, he too did not look his age; he had grown taller and sturdier recently, his fitness helped by his enthusiastic participation in rugby football at King Edward's School. They soon fell in love.

Her mother, Frances, had brought Edith up as a single parent, and died in her early forties in 1903, the year that Tolkien gained his scholarship to King Edward's School. What Edith had been told about her father is unclear. His name was known among the Bratt family, and presumably to her. Frances's family, who lived in Wolverhampton, had means, as boot and shoe makers.

Twenty years before, Frances had been in employment as a governess in the household of a paper dealer called Alfred Frederick Warrillow (1842–91) in Handsworth, not far from Edgbaston. The Warrillows had a daughter, Nellie, born 1875, who would have been taught by Frances. We know only the bare bones of events that ensued. The evidence clearly points to Warrillow getting Nellie's governess pregnant. Frances moved down to Gloucester to have the child away from the scandal, carrying the father's photograph with her. While Frances was pregnant, in 1888, Warrillow's wife, Charlotte, petitioned for divorce. After Edith's birth, Frances had moved back to the Birmingham area. There, at some point, she made contact with Warrillow, and certainly was in contact after his divorce, as she became the sole Executrix of his will.[13] Alfred Warrillow died in 1891, aged forty-eight, when Edith was two years of age. While there is no evidence that Warrillow provided Frances with any of the substantial money he left, in law she could benefit from his will as Executrix. He may have had liabilities: we know from newspaper reports that his company in earlier years had gone through financial difficulties. Humphrey Carpenter reveals that Edith had inherited land in "various parts of Birmingham", which produced a subsistence income.

Frances brought up her daughter with the welcome help of her niece, Mary Jane Grove, known as Jennie, who was only about five years younger than Frances. Edith was fourteen when Frances died. Her legal guardian, Stephen Gateley, sent Edith away to Dresden House School in Evesham, where she received a musical education and developed her love and talent for the piano. Some years passed before, having completed boarding school, Edith returned to Birmingham, to lodgings at the home of the Faulkners in Duchess Road. Although Mrs Faulkner was glad to have Edith's expert participation in her musical soirées, she decreed against her practising on the piano. According to Priscilla Tolkien many years later, based on some albums full of music her mother had carefully copied, Edith's tastes ranged "from classical music to the lighter ballads of the time". Priscilla remembered her mother telling her that she "would often work out her frustrations on the piano, playing something powerful and stirring, such as a Schubert Impromptu or a Beethoven sonata".

When Ronald and Hilary started lodging in Duchess Road, Edith was soon conspiring with them against "The Old Lady", as they dubbed her. The boys, who were constantly hungry under Mrs Faulkner's regime, were soon benefiting from contraband supplies. Edith had enlisted the frequent help of Annie Gollins, the maid, to smuggle morsels from the kitchen. Ronald and Hilary would lower a basket outside from their second floor room to receive the food. When The Old Lady was out, the boys would sometimes go to Edith's room for clandestine feasts.

The deception escalated, as Edith and Ronald took to meeting secretly (and therefore, of course, without a chaperone) in Birmingham tea rooms, a favoured one having a balcony above the busy city pavement. Their light-hearted rebellion was expressed by throwing sugar lumps from where they were seated onto the hats of those passing by. As a sugar bowl emptied, they would move to a new table. They got more daring by inventing their own whistle call. Hearing it at bedtime or early in the day, Ronald would rush to his window. By leaning out, he could see Edith at her window on the floor below. They sometimes had long talks through the night as a clock chimed the hours away. At this time, Edith's favoured name for him was John.

Nearly two years had passed since Edith and Ronald first met. Late in the autumn term of 1909, they decided upon a daring venture. It was not long before Ronald was due to take his examination for a scholarship to Oxford (King Edward's School had an exceptional record for placing its students in top universities). Edith was getting on in years; she would be twenty-one in a matter of months, some weeks after Ronald would be eighteen. The two conspired to cycle to the Lickey Hills, so familiar to Ronald, for an afternoon's outing. They would ride separately (Edith pretending to be visiting her cousin Jennie Grove) and meet up there, later returning singly. No one would dream that they had been together.

The lovers were noticed having tea together in Rednal, near Woodside Cottage and the Oratory retreat so beloved by Ronald. The sighting was mentioned to the caretaker at the retreat, who in turn gossiped to the cook at the Oratory. Thus the news reached the unsuspecting Father Francis. Ronald's guardian was concerned that his attentions towards Edith would distract him from his focus upon the looming

Oxford exams. Further research by Father Francis revealed something of the frequency of their clandestine meetings. There was nothing for it but to demand that Ronald and Edith stop their secret contacts.

At this point, Father Francis had not insisted that they did not see each other. Soon, Ronald was doubly depressed. Not only had his meetings with Edith come to an end, but he had failed to obtain the scholarship. The agony intensified when, in January 1910, his guardian found new lodgings for the brothers on the other side of the Edgbaston Road, at 4 Highfield Road. In desperation, Ronald decided that he and Edith must discuss what to do. They secretly caught a train into the countryside, and later visited a jeweller's shop in the city centre, where they bought each other gifts; Ronald's was a wristwatch for Edith's twenty-first, and Edith's a pen for his eighteenth. The next day, Edith's birthday, they celebrated in a teashop. Edith told Ronald she had decided to move to Cheltenham, not far from where she was born – some elderly friends had invited her to stay with them. Both agreed that this was a good plan. Unfortunately, they were seen together. Father Francis was eventually forced to be unambiguous. Ronald could not see, or even write to, Edith until his twenty-first birthday without his permission. His guardian was clearly concerned that his charge would fail to get into Oxford after another attempt at the examination, and what then?

There was no question of Ronald disobeying this explicit demand of Father Francis, the man who truly had been a father to him from before his mother's death. In the meantime, Edith found her new life in Cheltenham more congenial and fulfilling than she had expected. There could be no communications from Ronald, and in the course of time she became engaged to a young farmer called George Field, the brother of a friend.

3

Schooldays and the T.C.B.S.

It was Summer term 1911, and a year and a half had passed since Edith Bratt moved south to Cheltenham. Ronald had only been able to write to her twice, with Father Francis's permission. She had sent a blank Christmas card the previous December, blank to avoid getting Ronald into dangerous trouble. The threat of his losing his chance for Oxford University, and his loyalty to his guardian, meant the ambiguity of silence. He was to start his studies at Oxford in the autumn term.

Ronald still grieved over Edith, and had to make do with the male companionship of King Edward's School, although he did have intermittent contact with female relatives from both his father's and mother's sides, including his cousins Marjorie and Mary Incledon and his beloved aunt Jane Neave. Humphrey Carpenter speculates that, after Edith's departure, "All the pleasures and discoveries of the next three years – and they were vital years in his development, as vital as the years with his mother – were to be shared not with Edith but with others of his sex, so that he came to associate male company with much that was good in life."[1] This is perhaps an exaggeration: in later years, both Ronald and C.S. Lewis were caught in a social system within Oxford colleges where it was the norm for societies and friendships to be exclusively of the same sex. This was reflected in the ethos of the boys at the all-male King Edward's School, which aspired to send pupils to Oxford or Cambridge and had its Officers' Training Corps in the mainstream of school life.

The future holder of two distinguished Chairs at the university had passed the Oxford Scholarship examination the second time some months before, admittedly with little glory in the hothouse of achievement at King Edward's. His modest award would need supplementing by a school bursary, and the unfailing generosity of Father Francis. He should have got a much better scholarship, but had allowed himself a raft of distractions – frequent rugby matches, contesting in the school debating society (sometimes in Latin), drilling and field exercises with the Officers' Training Corps, but most of all, his absorbing fascination with languages, real or imagined, but preferably ancient. At the debating society, his maiden speech, daringly, was on a motion that was on the side of female emancipation, at a period without votes for women: "That this house expresses its sympathy with the objects and its admiration of the tactics of the Militant Suffragette". His delivery did not always match the strength of his arguments. People were wont to call him lazy, but this was far from the case. He fluctuated between being driven in his pursuits and succumbing to the allure of distraction. As so often in his life, the "distractions" sometimes turned out in the end to be the real thing for the vision that increasingly lit his path. This was certainly true of his delight in languages. C.S. Lewis got it right when he wrote: "Tolkien used to describe himself as 'one of the idlest boys Gilson (the headmaster) ever had'. But 'idleness' in his case meant private and unaided studies in Gothic, Anglo-Saxon and Welsh, and the first attempts at inventing a language."

In contrast to being lazy, Ronald took on many duties at the school and thoroughly carried them through, and had now gained the coveted privilege of Librarian, one of several boys to do so, mostly his close friends. He also took his rugby seriously, and had become an accomplished player. The previous year he had quite severely cut his tongue in the rough and tumble of the game. In later years he would be notorious for the indistinctness of his speech, and tended to blame this injury for it (even though he enunciated clearly when reading or reciting).

Over the years since his mother died Ronald gradually had made one friend after another. Since getting into the First Class in 1907, four years earlier, many of his friends had gradually joined him there as they reached seniority. The school had a complex organization at that time. Of the classes, the lowest was the Thirteenth, and some classes were unnumbered. King Edward's had a strong Classical emphasis, but there was the choice of a Modern (or Scientific) stream after a transitional class later in the school. Hilary had decided an academic course was not for him; his real desire, he eventually decided, would be to work on the land. He left King Edward's at the end of the summer term of 1910, when he was sixteen. Hilary had given his schooldays a good try. In those days, the majority of children – who were at neither grammar school nor public school – left at thirteen years of age, or even twelve, to pursue manual jobs.

The school library had become the focus of Ronald's informal group of friends. Flouting the school rules about no food or drink consumption in the library, the friends smuggled in the necessities for cups of tea and snacks. Years later, one of the group recalled that an abandoned tin of fish languished long on a library shelf until its stench assaulted the nostrils. Thus the "Tea Club" – which is what his clique of friends at first called themselves – came into being. Who were these friends?

One of Ronald's closest friends, and now in the Tea Club, he had got to know some time after returning to King Edward's after his spell at St Philip's School. Christopher Wiseman (who was the friend who remembered the decaying fish) was placed in the Fifth Class with Ronald in the autumn term of 1905. By the end of that term Ronald gained first place, and Wiseman second, in the class examinations. They became friends while playing rugby together, and their name for themselves was "the Great Twin Brethren". Though he was from a Methodist family well known in Birmingham, Wiseman found a great affinity with the Roman Catholic Tolkien. The two shared an interest in British archaeology, King Arthur, ancient scripts and languages, and a zest for discussing anything under the sun.[2] Wiseman was also sympathetic to Tolkien's experiments in invented languages. He was exploring the hieroglyphics and language of ancient Egypt out of his own interest. Like many of his friends, Wiseman combined seriousness with wit and humour. Humphrey Carpenter describes him as having "an energetically critical manner".[3]

Wiseman, unlike Ronald, had a strong commitment to modern science, although Ronald did have a formidable rigour in his technical work on language. Like numerous scientists to this day, Wiseman did not see this as contrary to his devout Christian faith. Accomplished in music, he thought Ronald rather tone deaf. As well as his ability in composing music (he was to set to music one of Ronald's early poems, "Wood-sunshine", for accompaniment by two violins, cello, and bassoon), he was an outstanding mathematician. Over sixty years after it was started, Wiseman described the origin of the Tea Club to Tolkien's official biographer, Humphrey Carpenter. It began, he said, "with very great daring". In the summer term of 1911, as usual, there were six weeks of exams.

> If you were not having an exam you really had nothing to do; so we started having tea in the school library.... We used to boil a kettle on a spirit-stove; but the great problem was what you were to do with the tea-leaves. Well, the Tea Club often went on after school, and the cleaners would come round with their mops and buckets and brooms, throwing sawdust down and sweeping it all up; so we used to put the tea-leaves in their buckets. Those first teas were in the library cubby-hole. Then, as it was the summer term, we went out and had tea at Barrow's Stores in Corporation Street. In the Tea Room there was a sort of compartment, a table for six between two large settles, quite secluded; and it was known as the Railway Carriage. This became a favourite place for us, and we changed our title to the Barrovian Society, after Barrow's Stores.[4]

The café in Barrow's Stores had opened in 1905, six years before, and was a feature of the city's centre.[5] The Barrovian

Society became abbreviated simply to the "B.S.", which in turn was combined with the original "T.C." (Tea Club) making the eventual title the "T.C.B.S.", for the group of like-minded friends.

Another of Ronald's friends at the core of the T.C.B.S. was Rob Gilson. Like Ronald and Wiseman, he was an early member. Robert Quilter Gilson was the son of the distinguished head teacher at King Edward's School. (Years before, Ronald had got permission from the Oratory Fathers to attend additional classes in New Testament Greek given by Rob's father.) Rob Gilson's mother had died four years before, in 1907, and his father remarried. The stepmother encouraged the boy's fervent and precocious interest in Renaissance painting and his flair for sketching and drawing. Ronald was no mean artist himself (as millions were to discover when reading *The Hobbit*). Visual art was just one of the interests the boys had in common, though they were not as close as Ronald was with Wiseman, and would soon become with another pupil, nearly three years younger than he was, Geoffrey Bache Smith.

Like all his friends at the core of the T.C.B.S., Rob Gilson was a persuasive debater. He was also deeply interested in theatre, both as actor and director. A few months after the beginning of the T.C.B.S., Gilson produced the annual school production with its inevitably all-male cast. It was of R.B. Sheridan's eighteenth-century play *The Rivals,* and Ronald, who travelled up after his first term in Oxford for it, gave a fetching performance as Mrs Malaprop, in keeping with his linguistic interests. Mrs Malaprop, as her name suggests, had the habit of applying words wrongly. Phrases or sentences like "he is the very pineapple of politeness" or "as headstrong as an allegory on the banks of the Nile" tripped off her unsuspecting tongue. From her, the term "malapropism" was added to the English language. Years later, C.S. Lewis (author of *The Allegory of Love,* on medieval love poetry) played with her "allegory on the banks" malapropism when he signed off a letter with "the alligator of love". Malapropriately, but in the spirit of fun, after the dress rehearsal the cast went off for refreshments to Barrow's Stores, striding in full costume up busy Corporation Street.

The King Edward's School Chronicle recorded:

> ... J. R. R. Tolkien's *Mrs Malaprop* was a real creation, excellent in every way and not least so in make-up. Rob Gilson as *Captain Absolute* made a most attractive hero, bearing the burden of what is a very heavy part with admirable spirit and skill; and as the choleric old *Sir Anthony,* C.L. Wiseman was extremely effective. Among the minor characters, G.B. Smith's rendering of the difficult and thankless part of *Faulkland* was worthy of high praise.[6]

The T.C.B.S. was to leave a permanent mark on Tolkien's character, which he captured in the idea of "fellowship", as in the title of the first volume of *The Lord of the Rings, The Fellowship of the Ring.* This recounts the choosing of those from the peoples of Middle-earth – Elves, Dwarves, Hobbits and men – who journey with and support the Ring-bearer, Frodo Baggins, on his quest to destroy the Ring of power. Tolkien's friends enjoyed and supported his growing interest in northern sagas and medieval English literature, and all things that were related in Ronald's mind to them. A milestone in

Ronald's discoveries, as he neared the end of his time at King Edward's, was the Finnish national epic poem, the Land of Heroes, or *Kalevala*. Not long after, he wrote that "the more I read of it, the more I felt at home and enjoyed myself".[7] In later years he would celebrate elements from the *Kalevala* in his story of a dragon slayer, "The Tale of Túrin Turambar", whose hero unknowingly marries his sister.

One important element of his friends' support was expressed in his discovery of the ancient Gothic language. This might not have seemed important to anybody but Ronald, but he could share his find among the friends who were to make up the T.C.B.S. This sharing echoed into the future, as Ronald's life work became centred upon languages like Gothic: this vocation included both his scholarly work and his fiction, which would eventually converge. He had come across a textbook called *A Primer of the Gothic Language,* by Joseph Wright, when he was about sixteen. It introduced him to an ancient Germanic language (related to early English, German, and others in the same family) of which only a few texts have survived. It also made him acquainted with the academic discipline in which he would not only teach, but would be an outstanding shaper. This was philology. Tom Shippey's book, *J.R.R. Tolkien: Author of the Century,* provides a clear and wide-ranging picture of the importance of philology as an area of study, demonstrated in Tolkien's work:

> In my opinion... the essence of philology is, first, the historical forms of a language or languages, including dialectal or non-standard forms, and also of related languages.... However, philology is not and should not

> be confined to language study. The texts in which these
> old forms of the language survive are often literary
> works of great power and distinctiveness....[8]

Ronald, many years later, described his encounter with Gothic in a letter, and said it was "a beautiful language" that reached the "eminence" of use in church liturgy.[9] Writing another time to his friend, the poet W.H. Auden, he disclosed that, in Wright's textbook on Gothic, he not only discovered "modern historical philology, which appealed to the historical and scientific side, but for the first time the study of a language out of mere love".[10] He also mentioned turning his Norse name, Ronald, and German name, Tolkien, into a Gothic form as "Ruginwaldus Dwalakoneis". In a lecture he confessed that "Gothic was the first [language] to take me by storm, to move my heart".[11]

Geoffrey Bache Smith ("G.B.S."), who acted in the Christmas term production of *The Rivals* at King Edward's, became another core member of the T.C.B.S. with whom Ronald could share such discoveries and, like him, was one of the genuine poets among them.[12] Their common desire to write, and to explore ancient literature, was increasingly to bring Ronald and Smith together. Just one of the many interests they shared was ancient roads and how they fell into ruin with the passing of time. Smith published some of his poems in *The King Edward's School Chronicle*. They talked about contemporary poets like W.B. Yeats and A.E. Housman, who influenced Smith's poetry. The conversation, however, was just as likely to veer towards early English ballads or the Welsh cycle of Celtic stories, *The Mabinogion,* concerned as it was with the mythological past of Britain. Smith commented on Ronald's poetry, including, when the time came, his earliest that related to Middle-earth. Because he was born nearly three years after Ronald, Smith was often two classes behind him, which explains why the two did not get to know each other until the production of *The Rivals*. His father had died in 1905, the year after Mabel Tolkien, leaving his widow, Ruth Annie Smith, with two sons. The fact that both had lost their fathers may have been part of the affinity that Ronald and Geoffrey were to find in each other.

Ronald made a distinction among his friends between those who were his closest and those who were in a kind of second division – they might, for example, have been a little too frivolous for his liking. (C.S. Lewis as a young man made similar distinctions and at first, when he got to know Tolkien as a colleague at Oxford, assigned him to the second class of friend.) Of the T.C.B.S., Wiseman and Smith were clearly of the first division, and Gilson eventually was recognized as such. There were other important friends Ronald had in the T.C.B.S., however, who seemed to have remained in the second division. These include a number of fellow pupils at King Edward's School who became members: Sidney Barrowclough, Thomas Kenneth "Tea-Cake" Barnsley, and two brothers, Wilfred Hugh Payton ("Whiffy") and Ralph Stuart Payton (the younger Payton, hence called "The Baby"). Barnsley was noted for his exuberance and fluent wit. His father was a Lieutenant Colonel (later Brigadier General) in the British Army. Barnsley's nickname ("Tea-Cake") presumably was in some way related to the T.C.B.S.'s Hobbit-like fixation with cups of tea and cake as well as a play on his initials, "T.K.". Wilfred Hugh, the elder Payton, was respected for his participation in a wide range of school activities, helping to lead them. He went on to Cambridge

University to read Classics, the same time that Ronald left for Oxford. The younger brother, Ralph Stuart Payton, was also respected and involved in many school clubs and societies, such as the shooting club, the school magazine, and the debating society. He eventually was to follow his brother to read Classics at Cambridge. Sidney Barrowclough was two or three years younger than Ronald. He participated in many of the same school activities as other friends who became members of the T.C.B.S., but he was never in its inner core. He eventually went up to Cambridge the same time as R.S. Payton – "The Baby" – also to read Classics.

A close friend of Ronald's, Vincent Trought, is a special case. With Ronald and Wiseman, he was one of the earliest members of the T.C.B.S. Like them, he was enthusiastic in supporting many school activities, and was notorious for his punning. He was considered slow of thought, perhaps because of speaking "often in a dreamy, weary fashion" in debate.[13] He was taken ill during the autumn term of 1911, when Ronald started at Oxford. After travelling to Cornwall to escape Birmingham's smoky air and convalesce, he died suddenly in January 1912, aged eighteen. This was only a few months after the inauguration of the club. His verse showed great promise. *The King Edward's School Chronicle* decided: "In poetry he found his most congenial means of expression, and some of his verses show great depths of feeling and control of language."[14] Ronald grieved, but had insufficient warning to travel the long distance to Cornwall from Oxford for the funeral. He was able to contribute to a wreath, however, from the T.C.B.S.

As well as school friends, teachers of course were very important in these formative years. On Ronald's school life at King Edward's, C.S. Lewis recalled that Tolkien "reported much good and little evil. His form master, George Brewerton (a 'fierce teacher'), introduced him to Chaucer in the correct pronunciation and lent him an Anglo-Saxon Grammar; and R.W. Reynolds introduced him to literary criticism." The teaching standards of the Classics alone in the school meant that Ronald and his friends could converse in Greek or Latin. As a result of his own private "hobbies", Ronald could astonish by breaking into fluent Gothic or early English (Anglo-Saxon).

George Brewerton was near to retirement age at the time Ronald left the school for Oxford, but seems to have lost none of his fire. He was the Classics master, in addition to teaching English Literature with knowledge and enthusiasm. As well as the loan of the grammar book on early English, Ronald particularly appreciated being introduced to Geoffrey Chaucer, one of England's greatest poets and storytellers, and on whom he would eventually become an authority. The correct pronunciation of Chaucer's Middle English by Brewerton as he read from *The Canterbury Tales* was particularly important to the boy. Ronald was already alert to huge changes in the English language in the past, and was beginning to see the enormous impact of the Norman Conquest in the eleventh century on early English language and literature. London-based Chaucer, he began to see, represented the success of Norman and Continental "romance" influences over against the efforts of other, more conservative, writers of the time who were still creatively employing older patterns of English. Ronald became endlessly fascinated by the turbulent changes in English language and literature in the fourteenth century in particular – the

intensely innovative period in which Chaucer and other
writers he relished composed their poems. Such were the
seeds that grew when he went up to Oxford, and that would
connect with his experiments in making up languages.

The other teacher mentioned by C.S. Lewis was
R.W. ("Dickie") Reynolds, who, like Brewerton, taught
English Literature to Ronald (the subject barely featured in
the official school curriculum). He also taught Classics and
History in the school. Before going into teaching, Reynolds
had written literary criticism for a well-read journal called
the *National Observer*. Ronald found his teaching of History
and the Classics "boring" and uninspired; it was obvious that
Reynolds' real enthusiasm was for literature. Humphrey
Carpenter speculates that the teacher's attempts to instil
an appreciation of style and taste in his pupils had the effect
of encouraging Ronald to write verse. One of his early
poems was called "Wood-sunshine", which was the poem his
T.C.B.S. friend Wiseman later set to music.[15] In it he wrote
of "light fairy things" who were "All fashion'd of radiance,
careless of grief". After leaving King Edward's, Ronald would
keep in touch with Reynolds, whom he found "immensely
interesting as a person", sending him pieces of his writing for
his comments, which he valued.

Ronald's final term at King Edward's School ended on
26 July 1911. The full leaving programme concluded with
a performance of Aristophanes' *The Peace*. Ronald was one
of those who played in the comedy, which was performed
in Greek, with the choruses set to popular tunes from the
music halls of the time. Aristophanes' play was originally
staged in Athens in 421 BC, at the time of the then ten-year-
old Peloponnesian War, when hopes were high that it would

soon end. Looking back, the choice of play seems very topical for a country just three years later to be hurled into a "war to end all wars". Then, weeks after leaving school, Ronald had a holiday in Switzerland that was to leave its enduring imprint on him.

Though perhaps not intended to be as such, the holiday celebrated Ronald's rite of passage from school to university. The arduous and sometimes dangerous trek across mountain ranges astonishing in height can be seen in hindsight as a symbolic journey from his schooldays to the adult vigours of study at Oxford and then war. Ronald could still remember it vividly over fifty years later, and what he saw was captured both in *The Hobbit* and *The Lord of the Rings*.

The adventure came about through a connection between Ronald's aunt Jane Neave and a family called the Brookes-Smiths. Aunt Jane at some stage had become a friend of the family, perhaps when she was warden of the women's college at the St Andrews University. Hilary Tolkien (now seventeen) was working on their Sussex farm in Hurst Green. The upshot was that Aunt Jane, Ronald, and Hilary accompanied the family to Switzerland during the summer of 1911. Jane Neave was to be responsible for food and cooking as they trekked and camped. The family consisted of James and Ellen Brookes-Smith, their daughters Phyllis (aged sixteen or seventeen) and Doris (aged fourteen or fifteen), and son Colin (aged twelve or thirteen). In addition there were "one or two unattached schoolmistresses"[16] and a couple or so more members of the party. Some of these joined the group during the holiday. A photograph in *The Tolkien Family Album* shows some of the party on the vast Aletsch Glacier, with Ronald sitting to the fore of the group beside one of the daughters. All in the party wield tall stout walking staffs, wear sturdy boots, and sport wide-brimmed hats as protection from the sun.

The travellers set off by ship from Harwich to Ostend in Belgium, then went on by train to Cologne, Frankfurt, Munich, and to Innsbruck in Austria, near the Swiss border, where their tour began. Travel now began to be more basic. It was by foot, and by train where necessary. They travelled a huge distance to Interlaken in Switzerland, presumably often by train. From here they were on foot, hauling their heavy packs, to Lauterbrunnen, much of the time following mountain paths and sometimes sleeping rough in barns. (The name "Lauterbrunnen" probably means "loud well" or "loud spring" or similar, giving rise to the reasonable idea that it inspired the River Loudwater – the translated name of the River Bruinen in Tolkien's stories – at Rivendell. Indeed, it is easy to imagine that the steep-sided valley of Lauterbrunnen had something to do with Ronald's later conception of Rivendell.) From here they eventually trekked past the giant peaks of the Eiger and the Mönch ("Monk"), and later the Jungfrau before negotiating a pass to Brig and the Rhône valley. These peaks inspired Ronald's imagination, emerging in later years in his drawings and descriptions of the Misty Mountains in Middle-earth. Nearly sixty years later he wrote in a letter: "I left the view of Jungfrau with deep regret: eternal snow, etched as it seemed against eternal sunshine, and the Silberhorn sharp against the dark: the Silvertine (Celebdil) of my dreams."[17]

From Brig they took to the mountains again, heading towards the giant Aletsch Glacier. They stayed in a chalet inn thousands of feet up, and went from there with guides on to the hazards of the glacier. That year there had been months of hot weather, melting the snow and exposing boulders and stones that were normally gripped securely by the ice. Ronald confessed that he "came near to perishing"[18]. As they filed along a narrow track with a steep slope of snow to their right and a vertiginous drop to their left into a ravine, dislodged boulders of various bulks began hurtling down the slope above them as they were dislodged from the melting ice. One passed between Ronald and an elderly teacher who was in front of him, who leaped forward with an exclamation just in time. It missed Ronald by a foot, making him weak at the knees. The incident helped to inspire the "thunderbattle" in chapter 4 of *The Hobbit,* which drives Bilbo, Gandalf, and the Dwarves to shelter in an apparently safe dry cave.[19] It possibly also inspired Tolkien's drawing of "The Mountain-path" in the same chapter. Ronald's journeys along narrow mountain paths past giant snow-headed peaks also appeared at appropriate moments in both *The Hobbit* and *The Lord of the Rings* – as when Frodo and his companions attempted in vain to cross the mountains beside the giant peak of Caradhras, and come close to perishing in a storm.

The rich store of memories of places and events that Ronald brought back from Switzerland is characteristic of how settings and names in the actual world transformed into stories and invented places in Middle-earth. He had an acute sense of place that matched his sensitivity to languages. Throughout his life, his experiences – often quite ordinary – constantly were to feed into his imagination, and thence into his fiction. He had the remarkable gift of being able to capture the quality of a landscape or even of a particular language in a way that his readers could experience. To use one of his own images, to come across the quality of a new language was like a lover of wine discovering a delightful vintage bottle and tasting it for the first time. As for the experience the reader of Tolkien enjoys, C.S. Lewis pointed to it when he remarked in another context that reading can enlarge our being by extending our experience – such is the power of words. He said, "In reading great literature I become a thousand men and yet remain myself. Like the night sky in the Greek poem, I see with a myriad eyes, but it is still I who see. Here, as in worship, in love, in moral action, and in knowing, I transcend myself, and am never more myself than when I do."[20]

4

Oxford and the dawn of a new life

It was the Christmas vacation of 1912. Ronald was now in his second year at Oxford, and was eagerly looking forward to his twenty-first birthday, just weeks away, when he could at last get in touch with Edith Bratt again. The prohibition of Father Francis would be over and, indeed, he would cease to be his guardian. The two had been apart for nearly three years. Part of that vacation he spent with the Incledons at Barnt Green, Worcestershire, as he had done the year before. Uncle Walter Incledon, Aunt May (his mother's sister), and cousins Marjorie and Mary were among his favourite relations. As usual a play was performed, and for this year Ronald had written one, entitled *The Bloodhound, the Chef, and the Suffragette*. As well as echoing the popular Sherlock Holmes stories, it reflected Ronald's preoccupations.

The play featured a lost heiress called Gwendoline Goodchild, who lodged in the same house as an impoverished student. The two had fallen in love, and the heiress would be free to marry on her twenty-first birthday in just two days' time. This was provided that her father did not track her down before then. Ronald did not take the part of the student, but the less obvious leading role of a famous detective called "the Bloodhound" – that is, Sexton Q. Blake-Holmes, who goes under the guise of an academic called Professor Joseph Quilter (borrowing one of the names of his T.C.B.S. friend, Robert Quilter Gilson). "The Bloodhound" was in search of Gwendoline. We don't know if Edith's mother had benefited at all from money left by Alfred Warrillow, the father Edith had been too young to remember. There was the inherited land, however, that Humphrey Carpenter mentions. It is clear nevertheless that the character of the lost heiress applied to Edith, and that of the poor student to Ronald. Though Ronald in his head knew he would be free to contact Edith, his heart still feared Father Francis's disapproval of his deeper intention – which was to marry his first love. It was daring of him to explore his preoccupations in front of his relations, but it is likely that he felt sure that they wouldn't make connections that were clear to him at the time.

Ronald didn't know it that Christmas, but the following year was going to be momentous for him. In the words of John Garth, at that period his "life reached its major personal and academic turning point".

Back in October 1911, the year before, Tolkien had entered Exeter College, Oxford, to read Literae Humaniores, one of the undergraduate schools, which was dominated by the Classics.[1] In less than two years, it would lead up to a marathon examination called Honour Moderations (or "Hon. Mods"), with another examination in the fourth, final year. He was driven to Oxford by car, a new experience for him, with another ex-pupil from King Edward's. Their driver was his former teacher, the kindly R.W. Reynolds. They would have taken the main road from Birmingham to Stratford-upon-Avon, Shakespeare's birthplace, and then on to Oxford via Chipping Norton, or an alternative route via the Vale of Evesham. The journey was about seventy miles.

The city, around the central area, then as now, is populated, often shoulder to shoulder, with beautiful college buildings belonging to the university. Each college also has its own chapel, quadrangles, and gardens, every one approached through an entrance watched over by the inevitable porters' lodge. The university is a federation of colleges, as are others, such as the universities of Cambridge and Durham. Exeter College is on Turl Street, connecting to Broad Street at the north end.

Ronald's accommodation was in "the Swiss Cottage" (since demolished) at that end of the street. Blackwell's Art and Poster Shop now occupies the spot. At the south end, Turl Street led into the High Street, where many of Ronald's lectures would take place in the Examination Schools. Broad Street gave access to the Taylorian Institute, a short walk away on St Giles, near the Martyrs' Memorial (soon known to Ronald and other freshmen as the "maggers memugger" in the curious student slang). At the Taylorian, others of his lectures were given. He had classes in addition, and one-to-one tutorials, where he would read an essay out to his tutor. The latter could take place in the tutor's own house or college rooms. Undergraduates wore a black gown and cap at all lectures and tutorials, as well as other academic occasions, such as exams and university ceremonies.

Oxford was small then, in comparison with its size now. Not far from its centre it was surrounded by a patchwork of small, hedged fields and old villages full of character. Unknown to Ronald, at that time a former Oxford bicycle maker, William Morris (later, Lord Nuffield), turned his attention to the manufacture of cars, setting up a factory in 1913 in Cowley, a suburb. Morris's genius was one of the forces of the dramatic changes Ronald was to see in his lifetime, that were to affect Oxford on a much smaller scale than what was happening in Birmingham and its districts, which were rapidly turning into an urban sprawl.

With little delay, Ronald was socializing boisterously and he also started his own undergraduate club, the Apolausticks, committed to "self-indulgence" (which, at that time, meant little more than youthful high spirits, but included some serious debate reflecting members' own interests). Literae Humaniores was heavily weighted with the whole range of classical study – Latin and Greek authors such as Aeschylus, Homer, Cicero, and Virgil, and also classical philosophy and history, taking in Plato, Tacitus, and others.[2] Ronald was allowed to choose a special subject, which in hindsight he must have seen as providential. This was in the subject he had discovered at grammar school – philology, the historic study of language and culture, which includes comparing languages. The title of his special subject was Comparative Philology. Despite the enjoyment Ronald had experienced at King Edward's, he lost most of his joy in the Classics under the rigorous Literae Humaniores syllabus. Years later he once confessed to C.S. Lewis: "My love for the classics took ten years to recover from lectures on Cicero and Demosthenes."[3] The situation was not helped for Ronald by the absence of a resident Classics tutor in Exeter College for some of his course.

His choice of special subject meant that Joseph Wright began tutoring Tolkien. It was this same Wright who had authored *A Primer of the Gothic Language* that Ronald had been delighted to acquire while still at King Edward's School. This Yorkshireman of humble origins (he started as a wool mill-worker when he was only six years old and taught himself to read at the age of fifteen) had, by a long struggle, become Professor of Comparative Philology at Oxford. One of his achievements was the six large volumes of his *English Dialect Dictionary*. Study of dialects was central to philology, and it was something that had always interested Ronald. When very young, Ronald's mother put him and his brother in dresses and kept their hair long, as was the custom with middle-class male toddlers. In rural Sarehole, the local children called them "wenches", a word that fascinated the young Ronald. As well as his studies with Joseph Wright, Tolkien also took up studying Welsh – the language that had enraptured him as a boy – and got immersed in Finnish. He began around this time to invent what would become Elven languages, one of which he was to call Quenya, or High Elven, based on Finnish, related to another one he eventually named Sindarin, based on Welsh. This was a more knowledgeable extension of his hobby of inventing languages, which he had enjoyed since he learned to write.

While Comparative Philology with Joseph Wright led Ronald to more and more delighted discoveries, he woefully neglected his main course of study in the Literae Humaniores school. Many put this down to laziness. His college warned him at one point that he might lose his Exhibition, the modest scholarship he relied upon to pay a good deal of his costs of study and subsistence, as well as the indulgences of his lifestyle. He also at this time neglected his Roman Catholic disciplines of the Mass and confession. In fact, Ronald allowed himself to be distracted by his involvement in a vast range of student activities, on top of his hobbies of inventing languages and exploring ancient scripts and languages, including what became a "wild assault" on the complexities of Finnish. He also was writing more and more poetry, which he was desperate to share with Edith, who had been part of his first audience for his poems in earlier days. He later told C.S. Lewis that his neglect of Classics at this time was in favour of "Old Norse, festivity, and classical philology".[4] Writing when only *The Hobbit* and *The Lord of the Rings,* and little else of his fiction, was known to the public, Lewis commented on Tolkien's invention of Elvish languages. He pointed out that this "was no arbitrary gibberish but a really possible tongue with consistent roots, sound laws, and inflexions, into which he poured all his imaginative and philological powers; and strange as the exercise may seem it was undoubtedly the source of that unparalleled richness and concreteness which later distinguished him from all other philologists".[5]

Ronald's exuberant fling with student activities was noticed by his peers. One, an ex-King Edward's pupil, laconically noted that "Tolkien, if we are to be guided by the countless notices on his mantelpiece, has joined all the Exeter [College] Societies which are in existence".[6] He also spent much time drawing, sketching, and painting. He was becoming more proficient in capturing places – buildings and landscapes – but still found it difficult to portray human figures. Part of the summer of 1912 was spent walking in Berkshire, enjoying its Downs and other countryside. He carefully sketched landscapes and villages, such as the countryside around Lambourn, south of the famous Ridgeway. Ronald drew details of the church at Lambourn, and thatched cottages at Eastbury.[7] This distinctive area is not all that far from Fawley, the setting of the fictional "Marygreen" in Thomas Hardy's famous novel, *Jude the Obscure* (where Jude's surname is Fawley, and Oxford, which can be viewed from certain places on the Downs, is called "Christminster").

Despite his overflowing life at Oxford, Ronald had not forgotten his friends in the T.C.B.S. Christopher Wiseman and Rob Gilson began studying at Cambridge in the autumn of 1912. Other members of the club joined the two a year later, leaving Ronald rather isolated in Oxford. These were T.K. "Tea-Cake" Barnsley and Wilfred Payton, later to be joined by Sidney Barrowclough and Ralph Payton. At this time, G.B. Smith, like Barrowclough and the younger Payton, was still at King Edward's School. Unlike the others, however, Smith's sights were on Oxford. Of the Cambridge contingent of the T.C.B.S., only Wiseman and Gilson seemed to represent the core values and seriousness of purpose of the club; Wiseman in particular found the superficial banter and frivolity of many of the others increasingly frustrating. Ronald would write to Wiseman and Gilson, and occasionally met up with them, but not as frequently as the other of the "Twin Brethren", Wiseman, would have liked.

That Christmas of 1912, as Ronald looked ahead to the next year, two major events challenged him. The first was to contact Edith once he reached twenty-one early in January, and the second was his end-of-February examinations, the first of the two he would have to sit to gain his degree based upon his studies in the Classics school of Literae Humaniores.

He had not seen his first love since 2 March 1910, getting on toward three years before. If he stopped to think about "Hon. Mods" at all, he would remember that he simply hadn't put in the required study. The college warnings could not be downplayed all the time. It was only in his special subject, Comparative Philology, that he was excelling.

Friday 3 January 1913, his birthday, eventually arrived. There was still a week of the vacation left before the Hilary (spring) term began, and Ronald was probably still staying with the Incledons. Precisely at midnight (when his coming-of-age was deemed to begin) Ronald sat up in bed and began a letter to Edith. The gist of it was simple: how he felt for her had not changed since their enforced separation, and he wished to marry her. The next day, the letter went off carrying his hopes. Within days, a reply came from Edith. He would have recognized the handwriting on the envelope. Upon reading it he learned for the first time that Edith had become engaged to a friend's brother, the farmer George Field. He was kind, she explained, and because of this was someone she felt would make a suitable husband. In the long separation, she wrote, she had begun to doubt Ronald, feeling that he would stop caring for her. George was the only young man she knew in her narrow Cheltenham circles. She was feeling that she was "on the shelf" (she was almost twenty-four). Edith did indicate however in the letter that now that Ronald had written and reaffirmed his love, this had made a big difference to her feelings.

It was clear to Ronald that he must see Edith without delay, and persuade her to give up George Field and agree to marry him. There were still some days left of the vacation before the intense pressures of the new term. Five days after first writing to Edith, on the Wednesday, he took a train to Cheltenham, where Edith met him at the station. They needed privacy for their conversation and walked into the countryside. There they talked, sitting between the pillars of a railway viaduct. Eventually, Edith decided to end her engagement with George Field and to throw in her lot with Ronald. He was a "poor student" like the character in the play that she had not seen. To the worldly-wise, his prospects didn't look good. Though the two of them would go through some difficult times in the future, they knew that each had chosen the other. In all their discussions of the future, then and during more than three years before their marriage, Edith made no mention of her illegitimacy.

They decided to keep their engagement secret for the time being, at least until Ronald's prospects looked up and they could make it public. An exception was Father Francis, whom Ronald was sure should be informed. He was rather full of foreboding when he wrote to his former guardian, whose financial generosity continued and was deeply appreciated. Ronald remembered Father Francis's hurt and anger over his clandestine meetings with Edith. Nevertheless, he made his decision to marry Edith quite clear. The situation now however was quite different. Ronald technically was no longer Father Francis's charge, but was of age. Though he had misgivings (he knew Ronald's faults as well as his strengths, and his lack of prospects), he concurred reluctantly with the wishes of Ronald and Edith. Their decision made no difference to his love. Indeed, he continued to play an important part in their lives.

The kind of thoughts that might have gone through Father Francis's mind in his worst moments of thinking through

Ronald's news were somewhat brutally expressed by Edith's "Uncle" Jessop, with whom she had lived, along with his wife, "Aunt" Jessop, all the time since leaving Birmingham. Upon hearing of Edith's engagement to Ronald, Jessop wrote to Stephen Gateley, Edith's guardian: "I have nothing to say against Tolkien, he is a cultured gentm., but his prospects are poor in the extreme, and when he will be in a position to marry I cannot imagine. Had he adopted a profession it would have been different." He could not imagine, of course, that he was writing about someone who would gain international eminence in the world of scholarship, and who would also become one of the highest-earning authors of his time!

Whether it was because Edith and Ronald decided not to make their engagement public yet is not clear, but at this time Ronald confided in none of his close friends about Edith. So neither university friends nor members of the T.C.B.S. heard the name "Edith" on Ronald's lips for a considerable period. Nevertheless, Ronald returned to Oxford after their mutual commitment to marry with a song in his heart and a spring in his step. He was able to face up to his shortfall in examination preparation more robustly. He was now accountable to Edith and to their joint future.

Miracles however failed to happen. When Ronald received his results, after sitting for many gruelling days of written papers, he found that he had only scraped a Second Class pass. An examiner recorded that Ronald's Latin prose paper was "largely illegible" and exclaimed that his one on Greek verse was presented in "filthy script!". In the few weeks before, when he had tried to catch up with four terms of neglect of his classical studies, he must have realized that he would fall short of what was expected of him. He had let

Edith down, as well as himself, as he needed a high result – a First Class grade – in order to hope for an academic career. A ray of light in the gloom of disaster was the result of his special subject, Comparative Philology. His written answers for this examination were virtually flawless, achieving a clear alpha grade.

Ronald's tutors, however, recognized his outstanding ability in philology. They suggested that he switch from Classics to the English Honour School, which would be far more compatible. Exeter College also generously offered to allow Ronald to keep his Exhibition, even though it had been given to help pay for his Classics degree course. The following (Trinity) term therefore found him studying in the English School.

The Oxford English School was a rigorous and demanding course, which would require two more years of study at Oxford. When Ronald looked through the syllabus, he became concerned that there would not be enough to occupy him "with honest labour" for two years! Because of his exploration of ancient languages and literature, particularly the Germanic family to which English belongs, he was already familiar with much on the syllabus. He soon found, however, that the rigours of the course and the high standard of teaching challenged him.

In the English School something of a battle was going on between the language and the literature sides, which would continue in various forms throughout Ronald's later career in Oxford. He was committed to respecting literary texts – they were to him things artistically created, complete in themselves, not simply a historic quarry for digging out words. Though he saw language and literature as being on a continuum, he was bent more on the language end of the scale. He could happily pursue the English course, weighted as it was towards philology, honing his skills. Describing the battle, Humphrey Carpenter wrote:

> On one side were the philologists and medievalists who considered that any literature later than Chaucer was not sufficiently challenging to form the basis of a degree-course syllabus. On the other were the enthusiasts for "modern" literature (by which they meant literature from Chaucer to the nineteenth century) who thought that the study of philology and Old and Middle English was "word-mongering and pedantry".[8]

The English School bumped along in an uneasy compromise.

Ronald threw himself heart and soul into his studies. The world of his extra-curricula activities and "hobbies" and the studies demanded of him by the university increasingly came together. That year he started a notebook with "Essays 1913" on the cover, which included what appear to be drafts, perhaps of essays he was composing for weekly tutorials.[9] The depth and confidence of them is remarkable – they are clearly work of the highest order. Some essays explore foreign influences upon early English, which changed the language sometimes dramatically, sometimes gradually, to a more modern form. These include "The Anglo-Norman Element in English", "The Language of Chaucer", and "Scandinavian Influences on English". Some are more generally historical, as with "The Origins of the English Nation" and "The Continental Affinities of the English Nation with its Bearing on Pre-Danish England". Many of his interests are explored, such as his "nationalism", that is, interest in what makes a nation such as England English. (This was far from the ugly nationalisms that were to result in the deaths of numerous millions of people in the twentieth century.) Ronald was very much interested in the great changes in English as a consequence of the Norman Conquest, with London-based Chaucer in a "modern" stream, while dialects like that of the West Midlands region were more conservative.

In the Michaelmas (autumn) term of 1913 Ronald was delighted that his close friend from the T.C.B.S., Geoffrey Bache Smith, entered the Oxford English School, attending Corpus Christi College, a short walk from Exeter College. Later, looking back on his first year, G.B. Smith wrote to Ronald (letter of 9 February 1916): "I never knew you until I went up to Oxford."[10]

Ronald was emotionally attached to his Suffield ancestry on his mother Mabel's side, which was associated with the West Midlands – in fact, he felt a strong emotional connection to all English regions that were, to him, "the Shire" of his stories.[11] Edith perhaps was linked emotionally with this same cultural home, as her mother, Frances, was from Wolverhampton, then in Staffordshire. This gave him a fervent interest in the West Midlands dialect and what of its literature has survived. This interest was over and above his trained appreciation and delight in both the language and literature in this dialect. Much of his future academic research and teaching would centre on the English of the West Midlands variety, especially in the fourteenth century. One "romance" of this period that captured him was the Arthurian story of *Sir Gawain and the Green Knight,* which he would one day translate into modern English. It is a beautifully crafted tale of a heroic quest, in which Gawain's virtue is tested by a warrior who is almost completely green in colour.

Such an emotional attachment as Ronald's to an ancient dialect of English is typical of the man. He did not work and create in an impersonal neutrality. While writing his essays for his tutors, attending lectures in the Examination Schools in the High Street or the Taylorian in St Giles, or throwing himself into student activity, Edith therefore was never far from his thoughts. After their commitment to each other, the subject of Christian faith had inevitably come up. Edith was an Anglican. While in Cheltenham, staying with the Jessops, her local parish church had been in the centre of her social life. She was well known among the cultured congregation for playing the organ, and participating in church activities. Her Anglicanism meant, however, that their marriage could not be blessed by Ronald's Roman Catholic Church. Edith was willing to take the step of converting – she loved and respected Ronald – but she suggested delaying until their engagement went public and the day of their marriage was closer. Ronald however was quite inflexible. He was tied into his emotional links to his Church – his mother and her suffering, the guardianship and protection of Father Francis, the shelter the Birmingham Oratory had provided for him and Hilary, the need for a firm, orthodox faith. The same tensions that made so many of his relations antagonistic to Roman Catholics also soured the perceptions of Catholics to Protestants and others. Ronald was particularly scathing of Anglicans. One of his closest friends, however, was a Methodist (Christopher Wiseman). Deep down, he had insecurities about faith.

The previous year he had lapsed in his Christian disciplines. He was increasingly feeling that many of his friends in the T.C.B.S. were losing moral commitment and steadfastness in favour of shallow frivolity. Edith voiced her own fears that Uncle Jessop would react very badly to her desire to marry a Roman Catholic. He made no secret of his anti-Papism. Ronald would countenance no hesitation, however; perhaps it seemed like a test of her commitment to him, as Humphrey Carpenter suggests.

Edith capitulated. Uncle Jessop reacted as she expected. He ordered her to leave as soon as she could find alternative accommodation. This was not simple. As a single woman with an appointed guardian, she needed a companion. Her thoughts turned to Jennie Grove, her considerably older cousin, who for many years had chosen to live with her mother Frances as she brought up Edith. After Frances's death, she was as a mother to her. Jennie was a tough and resourceful woman, even though only four feet eight inches in height due to a spinal injury in her youth. Soon she and Jennie were searching, and decided upon Warwick rather than a return to Birmingham or a place in Oxford. It was close enough to the great city to keep in touch with friends and relations, and also near enough to Oxford for Ronald to get there easily by train. Edith had given in over her Anglican churchmanship, but she could establish herself somewhat in her choice of home.

Warwick, with its castle and picture-postcard historic buildings, won the approval of them all. It suited Ronald in fact not to be too near Edith and Jennie as he established the pattern of his future life and work in his own choices at Oxford. Edith and Jennie eventually settled (with Jennie's dog, Sam) on a terraced house, 15 Victoria Street, within walking distance of the Roman Catholic church, St Mary Immaculate, and with a historic pub at the bottom of Victoria Street built in 1700.[12] Its sign announced that it was the Black Horse, which would not have gone unnoticed by Ronald. To her delight, Edith was able to have her own piano in the house, a piano that moved with her all the subsequent years of her life. She could play as her heart took her. Edith was to remain in Warwick with Jennie until she married Ronald in the early spring of 1916, about three settled years.

That summer of 1913, Ronald landed a summer job that was to remind him of the fragility of life. The job seemed an excellent prospect. His task was to escort and tutor on holiday in France three Mexican boys who were pupils at Stonyhurst College in Lancashire, a leading Roman Catholic institution. They would be escorted by two aunts who spoke almost no English. Ronald barely knew the basics of Spanish, and soon found that he could converse little in French, despite his written knowledge of it. He was held back by a dislike of all things French, a prejudice he would struggle with throughout his life. His emotional dismay about the Norman Conquest of England in the eleventh century operated like a reaction to a recent event, and coloured his perception of the contemporary French. He crossed the channel on 29 July with two of the boys (they were meeting up with the others in Paris), probably with some good intentions. But his Gallic experiences simply reinforced his disfavour. He simply could not forgive the devastating impact of the Norman invasion on his beloved English language and poetry.

The holiday started well enough. Ventura, José, and Eustaquio, the well-behaved and "jolly" boys, and their aunts

Angela and Julia, enjoyed the sights of Paris, as did Ronald. His enjoyment however failed to temper his judgmental attitude toward the French. His spirits rose when the elder aunt, Angela, declared their intention to continue the holiday in Brittany, with Julia remaining in Paris. This part of France was of great interest to Ronald, with his interest in Old Welsh, given the Celtic links between parts of westernmost Europe such as Galicia and Brittany with Cornwall and Wales. He felt rather deflated however when their destination, Dinard, near Saint-Malo, turned out to be a characterless seaside resort, replete with bathing machines and casual trippers. He found it all rather vulgar.

One day, Ronald was walking along a busy street with Angela and one of the boys. Without warning a car mounted the pavement and hit the aunt. Ronald helped in taking her to their hotel but within hours her acute internal injuries proved fatal. He found himself in charge of a difficult situation. Not only did he have to make all the arrangements over the body, including its transport to Paris by train, then later its return by ship to Mexico, but he felt very responsible for the boys. All the time he was in contact with a Mr Killion in England (apparently the boys' guardian, who had set up the original job for Ronald). Aunt Julia was intent on taking them home to Mexico as soon as possible, but Ronald felt that it would be better for the boys to go back to Stonyhurst College for the new term in September. After talking carefully with them, he contacted Killion about the boys' next move, and it was agreed that Ronald should bring them back to England, and give them a holiday in Bournemouth for two weeks before they returned to Stonyhurst. During the last part of August, before embarking for England, Ronald took great care to provide the boys with reading, and a board and pieces for them to play draughts. When Ronald eventually got to Edith in Warwick, he vowed that he would never take on such a job again!

Ronald the orphan had been reminded of death a year and a half earlier with the passing of his close T.C.B.S. friend, Vincent Trought. Now, in France, he had seen violent injury, quickly followed by death. Though the aunt Angela was not of course a friend or family member, he saw the impact of her death upon the three boys that he had in his charge. Death was not a reality that he could escape from; it would be a theme that haunted his fiction. He little suspected what the immediate years would bring.

5

The shadow of war

Ronald Tolkien continued to pursue his studies in the university English School with enthusiasm and thoroughness. He was able to explore the great Old English poem, *Beowulf,* about a northern hero whose achievements include slaying a dragon and other supernatural creatures. This epic poem was to become not only a major part of his future scholarship but also a central inspiration for his fiction. The same was true of many of the medieval romances that he studied, such as tales from Chaucer's famous *The Canterbury Tales,* and *Sir Gawain and the Green Knight*, a story from the days of King Arthur. Many of the texts he studied referred to biblical material, such as paraphrases of Scripture, sermons, and devotional writings. Some were bestiaries (collections about beasts), often concerned with magical creatures, and others riddles. (The prevailing concept then of what literature is was much broader than in many university English departments a hundred years on.) Tolkien was receiving a thorough grounding in the thought and imagination of a vast period that was to underpin his fiction. (This was also to happen with C.S. Lewis, who would also study in the Oxford English

School, starting in 1919.) When, in the future, people read his yet undreamed *The Hobbit, The Lord of the Rings,* and accounts of the earlier ages of Middle-earth, they would be stepping into that medieval vision of reality. It would, of course, be a version by a modern storyteller, but the splendour of the ancient period Tolkien was studying in the English School in Oxford would be retained.

Warwick remained in his mind, and he visited Edith there often, though this did not stop him keeping in contact with the T.C.B.S. – but not as often as Christopher Wiseman wished. He considered himself and Tolkien very much at the core of what the T.C.B.S. stood for, guardians of its guiding vision. Tolkien paid other visits too, when he could, seeing Hilary and other relations like his aunt Jane Neave. Edith's presence in Warwick created in him an emotional attachment to the town, which he explored imaginatively in his poetry and burgeoning art – both drawings and watercolours. He got to know its often quaint streets and alleys, its Westgate (near the Catholic church of St Mary Immaculate), historic buildings, river bridge, trees, gardens, and its magnificent castle, on a hill above the slowly passing River Avon. One of his drawings was made on the occasion when he took Edith punting, which he entitled *Warwick Castle Seen from Under the Bridge.*[1]

When visiting Warwick, Tolkien stayed at various venues. He and Edith in the years of enforced separation had grown apart in many ways. Being together in Warwick, where Edith was relishing her independence and the sheer domesticity of her situation, on some occasions brought out tensions. Edith also at times found the constant proximity of older cousin Jennie Grove irritating – according to Humphrey

Carpenter, "they often got on each other's nerves". Tolkien was never there for long periods, what with his studies, and other activities even during the university vacations. Despite irritations, both Tolkien and Edith seemed to have been reasonably comfortable with Jennie Grove's presence, and she would remain part of their lives throughout future decades. Such frictions were minor compared with the sudden, unwelcome intrusion of war.

On 4 August 1914, Germany invaded Belgium, and Britain declared war. Between 1914 and 1918 the war took in most of Europe, along with Russia, the United States (after 1917), the Middle East, and other areas of the world. Before being dwarfed by the savagery of the Second World War, it ranked as one of the most destructive and horrific wars in history. It resulted in the collapse of four imperial dynasties and revolution in Russia, and created the conditions that eventually led to the Second World War. It was the first global war in the history of humanity.

Two weeks or so after the outbreak of war, later in August Tolkien made his way to Warwick to be near Edith. For a week, or possibly longer, he stayed at the White House, in Northgate, near to where Edith and Jennie Grove were living in Victoria Street. There was much that he and Edith had to discuss, affecting their future. They were both trying to grasp the implications of war. Neither of course had the benefit of hindsight. Many people then thought that the conflict would not last long. Hilary Tolkien was preparing to enlist, or had already, as a private (reflecting his status as a land worker). In contrast, if Ronald enlisted, he would be an officer. Hilary joined up with the 16th Battalion of the Royal Warwickshire Regiment as a bugler. He was to serve in France for most of the war, and be injured several times. Hilary's decision to enlist added to the pressure upon Tolkien to do the same. Many of his fellow students at Oxford were leaping into the torrent of volunteers, driven by idealism to serve king and country.

The enlistment of his close friends from the T.C.B.S., G.B. Smith and R.Q. Gilson, was to be one of the hardest blows. Rob Gilson signed up with the Suffolk Regiment (the 11th Cambridgeshire Battalion) in late November. Soon after, Geoffrey Smith joined the Oxford and Buckinghamshire Light Infantry, and was then posted to the 19th Lancashire Fusiliers. He travelled west to Penmaenmawr in North Wales for training. Tolkien lost the familiar company of his friend at Oxford.

During the First World War, one out of every eight men drawn into the conflict died.[2] The large number of those enlisting from Oxford and Cambridge Universities, along with others from Britain's social elite, had a very much higher death rate than the average recruit. This was because most became junior officers, leading assaults and operations against the enemy, making them particularly vulnerable.[3] In the twelve months alone up to the end of July 1916, forty-two ex-pupils from King Edward's School, Birmingham, were to die.[4]

Soon after seeing Edith in Warwick, Tolkien made his way to a farm in Gedling, then in the countryside east of Nottingham, just sixty miles away. (The farm has since disappeared into the urban spread.) The Brookes-Smiths, with whom Tolkien had holidayed in Switzerland, by 1913 had bought two farms in Gedling village. Both his aunt Jane Neave and Hilary worked at one of them, Phoenix Farm, his aunt utilizing her science degree. This was a significant moment in Tolkien's life. Here at Phoenix Farm he announced that he was to defer enlisting – he told Aunt Jane that he intended to complete his Oxford degree first. As he anticipated, the expectation of his relatives was that he should join up without hesitation, postponing his studies like so many of his peers. But Tolkien was taking a longer view, now that he would soon be married to Edith. He had responsibilities to more than himself. Besides, he would have his degree in the bag by the next spring. It was crucial that he got a First Class grade to ensure a career in the academic world, and therefore to confirm his prospects before marrying. To break off his intensive studies now with the distractions of military life could mar his chances. He no doubt remembered his poor result in the Classics examinations. Perhaps he felt insecure, too, over Edith, not wanting to lose the momentum towards marriage. Tolkien had much to preoccupy his thoughts.

This did not stop his ever-active imagination from working, however. While he was at Phoenix Farm, he had in his mind the eighth-century poem by Cynewulf, *Crist* (Christ), which was on his syllabus to study. When previously working through what he found was a rather dull text in Oxford, he had become excited by some lines. In the Old English of *Crist* he read:

> *Eala Earendel engla beorhtast*
> *ofer middangeard monnum sended.*

This can translate as "Hail, Earendel, of angels the brightest, sent over middle-earth to mankind!" He was fascinated by the name "Earendel", which took him back in time, he felt, "far beyond ancient English".[5] He discerned a hint of a buried mythology in the Old English language.

By this time, he may have decided that every language has its own ancient mythology built into it. Also (and just as important) he grew to believe that it is inconceivable to have a mythology without language, or language without a mythology. One of the significant thinkers of our time, George Steiner, spoke of what Tolkien discovered as a young man, when he started creating languages. "Very soon Tolkien made his great discovery: the basic design of a grammar is a lifeless thing without a mythological content, without the image of a partly real and partly imaginary world which gives human speech its vital mixture of communications and secrets."[6]

Tolkien was not using the idea of "mythology" in the sense of being untrue, but as being about something believed or, at least, once believed. A language carries a particular view of the world. This is how the Oxford English Dictionary puts this meaning of "mythology", out of several: "3b: A body or collection of myths, esp[ecially] those relating to a particular person or thing, or belonging to a particular religious or cultural tradition." In later years, he said that the lines from the poem *Crist* that inspired him were "rapturous words from which ultimately sprang the whole of my mythology".[7]

While at Phoenix Farm the reference to the mysterious "Earendel" took wings. It inspired the very beginning of Tolkien's own mythology, which would one day be a connected body of legends and stories, including an account of the creation of the universe in which Middle-earth is located. Though still unfocused, he started writing about Eärendil the Mariner (there are several alternative spellings of Eärendil): "Éarendel sprang up from the Ocean's cup/In the gloom of the mid-world's rim…".[8] Dimitra Fimi says that "Tolkien's mythology starts to emerge from this point onwards".[9]

The story of Eärendil's life and voyage is one of the earliest elements in Tolkien's fiction. It slowly evolved over the long years that he was to spend developing the whole world of Middle-earth, and was never completed. The main bones of the story are clear, however, as is the importance that Tolkien attached to it as part of "The Silmarillion" – the stories and accounts that form the rich background to *The Hobbit* and *The Lord of the Rings*.

Eärendil has a strategic role in bringing "The Silmarillion" to its conclusion. His descendants provide the main links to the persons in the tales of later Ages, particularly in the events recounted in *The Lord of the Rings*. It is a quest story, in which Eärendil represents both Elves and men. He seeks a seaway back to Valinor, the Land of the Valar (the angelic powers). He is an ambassador, interceding for the rescue of the Elves and men in Middle-earth. Eärendil carried one of the bright gems from the dawn of Middle-earth, a Silmaril. After gaining relief for those in distress from the evil of the fallen Vala, Morgoth, he "sailed out of the mists of the world into the seas of heaven with the Silmaril upon his brow". His star in the sky (the Morning Star, or Venus) was a sign of the providence of Ilúvatar, the creator of all, providing hope.

Upon his return to Oxford for the new term Tolkien found Exeter College, and indeed the whole university, quickly emptying of students and some staff as they went off to train for war. As there was as yet no conscription, in theory enrolling was entirely voluntary. To his relief he found that he could do some officer training while continuing his studies. The pressure on him to abandon his studies had been intense, and this possibility immediately cheered him up. He continued to be sanguine about the training even when he found himself participating in drills in the University Parks nearby, and attending weekly military lectures, and sessions in map reading and signalling when he had free afternoons. The drills were frequent: on Monday mornings from 9 to 10 a.m., and on Wednesday, Friday, and Saturday afternoons from 2 to 4.30 p.m. It kept him free of a common lethargy that many students blamed on the river-basin dampness in Oxford.

One of his college friends, Colin Cullis, suffered poor health, and so was prevented from enlisting. The two decided to find "digs" rather than stay in college accommodation. They found rooms at 59 St John Street, quite near the Taylorian Institute, where some lectures were held. Tolkien soon found the digs were "a delicious joy compared with the primitive life of college".[10] G.B. Smith remained in Oxford that term, awaiting his commission. Tolkien benefited from his comments on his fledgling poetry. At one point, Smith suggested that his writing might improve if he read more widely in English Literature, instead of confining himself to Old and Middle English texts.

On top of his university studies and officer training, Tolkien at this time retold much of the story of Kullervo from the Finnish poetic epic, the *Kalevala*, before abandoning it uncompleted. He filled twenty-one sides of foolscap, covering about two-thirds of the story. The story was not far removed from his slowly emerging body of tales and annals of Middle-earth; in later years he transformed the story of Kullervo into his vivid and powerful tale of the tragic dragon-slayer, Túrin Turambar. Tolkien wrote in the style of William Morris, in whose book *The House of the Wolflings* he had found an episode from the Kullervo story. Morris had been prominent in the Victorian Arts and Crafts Movement, and interspersed verse and prose to tell sagas set in ancient times, such as *The Roots of the Mountains.* Morris was a former student at Exeter College. He translated Icelandic tales and sagas, much to Tolkien's interest. Tolkien started to attempt translations himself, inspired by his studies of Old English texts. Earlier that year, when he won the Skeat Prize for English, Tolkien had used some of the money to buy three books by William Morris, including *The House of the Wolflings*.

In a curious way, the climate of war was having an invigorating effect upon Tolkien's imagination. Perhaps it was because war heightened the importance of ordinary life. Elements like love, friendship, enjoyment of art, and the free pursuit of knowledge, worship, and leisure, even if hard-won in poverty, in representing peace stood in contrast to war. Those enlisting thought that they were out to defend all that meant home and peacetime. Tolkien's creativity arose out of the ordinary, which is why the Shire, and its protection, is at the heart of *The Lord of the Rings,* standing for the wider protection of the human itself. Years later he was deeply pleased when, in another wartime, author and editor Charles Williams, a future friend, commented on the emerging chapters of his story in this way. Tolkien reported in a letter that Williams saw the centre of *The Lord of the Rings* "in freedom, peace, ordinary life and good living" rather than "in strife and war and heroism (though they are understood and depicted)".[11]

The war also had the effect of focusing the purpose of the T.C.B.S. It had passed beyond its initial existence as a school club into something that clarified what university study, poetry writing, art, and architecture were all about. At least it did for some of the members. Others seemed only to see the frivolous side of things. While Christopher Wiseman studied at Cambridge, he thought a lot about the T.C.B.S. and its possible function not only in members' lives but also in wider society and culture. G.B. Smith, one of the core members, was soon to interrupt his studies with war service, as was Rob Gilson. Wiseman worried about the impact of military life and war upon Gilson's sensitive nature. Then he had the idea of calling a "Council of London". His parents had moved to London, and his new home was large enough to accommodate the four core members, who were all that he wanted at the meeting.

Wiseman persuaded G.B. Smith, Rob Gilson, and even Tolkien, whose attendance at T.C.B.S. gatherings had been poor, to meet in Wandsworth in the Christmas vacation of 1914 for the "Council of London". This event was to have a far-reaching effect on the direction of Tolkien's thinking and imagination. In fact, it changed all four in various ways. Some weeks before the gathering, Tolkien responded to a letter from Wiseman expressing his fears about the future of the T.C.B.S. In his view, Wiseman's fears were in part due to the fact that the four had only been able to meet when less sympathetic members were present. The fears were also due because "the great twin brotherhood" (that is, he and Wiseman) hadn't been able to get down to bedrock issues like Christian faith, human love, and patriotism, which were the forces that moved them. They shared a "vitality and fount of energy" that led to the very inception of the T.C.B.S. and which could shake the world.[12]

Over the weekend of Saturday 12th and Sunday 13th December, the four friends clustered around a gas fire in a small upstairs room, talking through the haze created by their pipes. According to Wiseman the magic happened. Whenever they met together they felt "four times the intellectual size". As the T.C.B.S. had developed in the school years, and now beyond, a vision was clarifying. The four began to sense that they might make a contribution to the world. What such an achievement might be centred on their individual gifts. Gilson's inclined to architecture and art. Smith's was in poetry. Wiseman's were not clear. For Tolkien, the "Council of London" opened a door, gave him a "voice for all kind of pent up things". It was then that he decided he was a poet. He regarded the weekend "as a turning point in his creative life" – to take John Garth's words from his brilliant study of Tolkien and the First World War. [13] For Wiseman and Tolkien, at least, the light they might take into an increasingly dark world lay in their Christian faith and world view. Their vision, however, was shaped by its time – the context of 1914, and escalating war. But there was something pure in it that could light up any culture. In the meantime, the young Tolkien saw their vision as what he had put on the agenda for the meeting: religious faith, human love, duty to one's country, and a nation's right of self-rule.

With the focus provided by Tolkien's agenda, the four worked to define the essence of their "fellowship", as perhaps Tolkien might have described the club in later years. John Garth captures the purpose that they perceived:

> The society existed to nurture and amplify each
> member's creative powers, which should be used to
> restore various neglected values to a decadent and

mechanized world – among them (as outlined by
Tolkien) religious faith, human love, patriotic duty and
the right to national self-rule. He felt the T.C.B.S. "had
been granted some spark of fire – certainly as a body
if not singly – that was destined to kindle a new light,
or, what is the same thing, rekindle an old light in the
world," and he likened the group to the Pre-Raphaelite
Brotherhood. It would work through inspiration, rather
than didacticism and confrontation. Each member
hoped to make his own mark on the world (Smith
through poetry, Gilson through the visual arts), but
Tolkien seems to have been tacitly viewed as the guiding
spirit of the group.[14]

The four realized that they had to take a painful step in order
for the T.C.B.S. to survive in its essence, and to go valiantly
forward. It would be necessary to purge it so that only the
four remained. Thus it was that their friends the two Payton
brothers, "Tea-Cake" Barnsley, and Sydney Barrowclough
were no longer considered part of the club.

Time sped on. Tolkien, invigorated by the mutual and
renewed vision of the T.C.B.S., worked through the final
terms of the English School. He also wrote poetry that was
maturing and surer in expression. Smith read the verse and
sent comments from his training camp. One lovely short
poem that Tolkien wrote about Edith included a sustained
image of two woodland trees that were tangled together
as they grew, nurtured by the earth of Life in which they
were deeply rooted. In Tolkien's world of Middle-earth a
symbol of two trees, associated with the sun and the moon,
is at its heart. In this early poem, the trees are associated

specifically with Edith and him. Edith would continue to play an important part in his imagination, in subtle ways.

Eventually Tolkien had his First Class honours degree in English. He received the news on 2 July 1915 from a list that had been posted – an announcement of his success appeared in *The Times* the next day. His future career was secured; his prospects were good. He could marry Edith. Tolkien however had already requested a commission days before in an army in which very many, more than he could have imagined, would perish. He had requested to join the 19th Battalion of the Lancashire Fusiliers (G.B. Smith's battalion). All he could do now was await his orders. Smith had sent him a long shopping list of the gear he would need, which he would have to buy out of his own pocket.

6

War and loss

By marrying Edith, Tolkien brought her settled stay in Warwick to an end. As Mrs Tolkien she would follow her husband as he was posted here and there for his training, and faithful Jennie Grove would accompany her. The ceremony took place in the church of St Mary Immaculate in Warwick, after an early Mass. The priest there, Father Murphy, led the service.

They married on Wednesday 22 March 1916, after Tolkien had been in army training for eight months. (A Wednesday was chosen to commemorate the day of the week in which they had renewed their promises to each other in Cheltenham, three years before.) The couple had decided to take the step before Tolkien was despatched to France, a summons that was imminent. News from the battlefront made the once unthinkable scale of casualties clear. They both knew that he might never return. Also they were aware of how long they had waited to join themselves in holy matrimony. Tolkien was now twenty-four, and Edith twenty-seven. They had little ready money between them; he had his army pay and Edith her modest allowance.

Tolkien had finally pushed himself to let Father Francis know that they were to marry. It was by then only around two weeks before the event. He could not forget the priest's prohibition six years earlier against seeing or writing to Edith. Father Francis responded by heartily wishing him and Edith "every blessing and happiness" and saying that he would marry them in the Oratory in Birmingham. Tolkien then had to admit that the arrangements were already made, and that the wedding would be in Warwick.

The shadow of the past thus meant that the ceremony was performed not by Father Francis, but rather by a priest neither of them warmed to. The shadow also touched the simple act of signing the register after the wedding. As Edith was about to sign, she realized that her father's name was required. She hadn't told Tolkien that she was illegitimate; only that her father was dead. Flustered, she wrote in the name as "Frederick Bratt", who in fact was her uncle. The box for "Rank or Profession of Father" she left blank. When she confessed the truth afterwards to her new husband, he was gentle and understanding. For a week, they honeymooned together in the popular seaside resort of Clevedon, Somerset. As part of that holiday they visited the renowned Cheddar Gorge and Caves, which, like Warwick already, would become part of Tolkien's imagined landscapes.

Since enlisting in the infantry, the trainee officer had been based first and briefly in Bedford, and then had been posted to a camp near Lichfield, in Staffordshire. He was disappointed not to be able to be in the 19th Lancashire Fusiliers with G.B. Smith, with whom he felt an increasing affinity. Tolkien began with the lowest officer's rank – that of temporary second lieutenant. With a fellow officer he bought a motorcycle (an AJS model popular at the time), which allowed him more easily to visit Edith in Warwick during the time leading up to their wedding. At the time, the other T.C.B.S. members – G.B. Smith, Rob Gilson, and Christopher Wiseman – were able to meet up with him for a "Council of Lichfield". This was on Saturday 25 to Sunday 26 September 1915. They met at the large George Hotel in the city centre, Tolkien having made the arrangements. Lichfield is the birthplace of Dr Samuel Johnson, who single-handedly compiled the first truly authoritative English dictionary, and described the place as "a city of philosophers" because of its intellectual and cultural life at the birth of the industrial revolution. It is appropriate therefore that the T.C.B.S. "philosophers" met here. One of them would one day work on a dictionary even more ambitious than Johnson's (though not single-handedly). All four were now officers in training and Smith, Gilson, and Wiseman travelled from Salisbury Plain, Marston Green (Gilson's home, then a village near Birmingham), and Greenwich respectively. Unknown to them, it was to be the last time all four met up. Smith wrote afterwards that it was full of the kind of "delightful and valued conversation which ever illuminates a council of the TCBS".[1] One topic of conversation undoubtedly would have been an anthology, *Oxford Poetry 1915,* brought out later in 1915 by Blackwell, which contained verses by Smith and Tolkien of the T.C.B.S., and also included contributions by Aldous Huxley and Dorothy L. Sayers, among others.

"Goblin Feet", Tolkien's contribution, was later published in various collections. He had written the verses in the spring, partly to please Edith. The poem featured tiny fairy goblins with lamps, and flying "flittermice", among the flowers and trees at dusk. The way he imagined the Fair Folk was very different from his mature depiction of Elves in *The Lord of the Rings,* and in *The Silmarillion,* though there are perhaps hints of it in the Wood Elves of *The Hobbit.* In the future, he was to depict Elves as larger than human, and spiritually superior.

A few months later G.B. Smith, in a trench dugout on the Western Front, found strength and sustenance in more developed verse by his friend.[2] Tolkien had sent him a poem called "Kortirion Among the Trees". Kortirion represented Warwick in the early stages of Tolkien's mythology, and was the chief town, complete with tower, in a region of elms (Warwickshire) on the Lonely Island (England). The island was called Tol Eressëa. Both place names were Elvish, in the new language he was creating. Kortirion was on a hill, had a gate that was built long ago, winding streets, and alleys with walls that cast their shade. There were colourful peacocks, and a river gliding past on its way to the sea. Kortirion's glory lay in its trees – elm, beech, willow, poplar, and yew. The poem's tone is that of an elegy, beautifully capturing, as the seasons pass, a quality of decline, the approach of ruin, and the fading of something extraordinarily beautiful. That beauty was from the Elves, whose traces still could be found in Kortirion. Smith wrote fervently about the poem to John Ronald, as he called Tolkien. He could see some meaning in being in the midst of war:

> I carry your last verses… about with me like a treasure…. I don't care a damn if the Bosch drops half-a-dozen high explosives all round and on the top of this dugout I am writing in, so long as people go on making verses about "Kortirion among the Trees" and such other topics – that is indeed why I am here, to keep them and preserve them …[3]

Perhaps Smith could be called Tolkien's first fan!

Tolkien's picture of an England where the fairy folk are fading away is somewhat reminiscent of Rudyard Kipling's remarkable *Puck of Pook's Hill* (1906), which was very popular at the time. In that, tales from English history are told to two modern children, some by Puck, a mysterious figure representing those fairies who still remain. Other stories are told by figures Puck magically brings from the past.

In December 1915 Tolkien was moved to Brocton Camp, on Cannock Chase. This was a moor, then a vast area of open heathland and some natural woods, including oaks hundreds of years old. Much of the area had been turned over to the army by Lord Lichfield and used for training camps. Brocton Camp, named after a nearby village, was effectively a small town of regimented large huts, roads, and railway lines, which had its own shops, bank, post office, sewage system, and a water tower. Much of Cannock Chase has reverted to its natural state since, and there is an extensive plantation of pines, with little trace of the vast training camps of the First World War. Tolkien received mail there regularly from the other members of the T.C.B.S., G.B. Smith and Rob Gilson from different parts of France, and Christopher Wiseman from HMS *Superb* (he was serving with the Royal Navy). While in camps in Staffordshire there was often plenty of empty time between military training activities for Tolkien to work on his "hobby" of developing his increasingly complex invented language of Elvish, with its two variants, and writing verse. The poetry was increasingly connected to the mythology that was opening up in his imagination. He was laying the foundations for his body of legends (what he later called the "legendarium") concerning Middle-earth.

G.B. Smith wrote again to Tolkien on 3 February 1916, as he got ready for a hazardous patrol that night in No Man's Land (the area between the opposing lines of trenches). If he didn't have a premonition of his own death, he at least knew that it was quite likely. He blessed and in effect prayed for his friend, and the aspiring poet was confident that Tolkien could be his voice:

> My dear John Ronald, publish by all means. I am a wild and whole-hearted admirer [of your poetry], and my chief consolation is, that if I am scuppered tonight – I am off on duty in a few minutes –there will still be left a member of the great TCBS to voice what I dreamed and what we all agreed upon. For the death of one of its members cannot, I am determined, dissolve the TCBS. Death is so close to me now that I feel – and I am sure you feel, and all the three other heroes feel, how impuissant it is. Death can make us loathsome and helpless as individuals, but it cannot put an end to the immortal four!...
>
> Yes, publish... You I am sure are chosen, like Saul among the Children of Israel. Make haste, before you come out to this orgy of death and cruelty ...
>
> May God bless you, my dear John Ronald, and may you say the things I have tried to say long after I am not there to say them, if such be my lot.[4]

Weeks after the wedding in March, Edith with Jennie Grove moved from Warwick to Great Haywood, a pretty Staffordshire village on the edge of Cannock Chase within walking distance of Tolkien's camp. There they rented furnished rooms, perhaps in property belonging to St John the Baptist Roman Catholic church.[5] Tolkien had time to become familiar with the village and its approaches. The old village is little changed today, though surrounded by new developments. One can walk under the railway bridge, as Edith and Tolkien would have done, and onto the many-arched and narrow Essex Bridge, very near the confluence of the Rivers Trent and Sow. After crossing this ancient packhorse bridge, and on the right, the view opens up across its parkland to the distant Shugborough Hall, with its dominant frontage, including a columned terrace, and its symmetrical wings. It has eighty chimneys, which may have impressed Tolkien, for in his stories of the time he writes of "the House of a Hundred Chimneys" near the Bridge of Tavrobel (a place in the early form of his mythology that is inspired by Great Haywood). The bridge stands near the meeting of two rivers in these stories.[6] Shugborough Hall was then the home of Lord Lichfield. Great Haywood provided some pleasant interludes as Tolkien and Edith awaited his summons to the battlefront.

Tolkien decided to specialize in signals, perhaps as a reaction against learning the skills of running through someone with a bayonet, grenade throwing, and killing in general. (It would also increase his chances of survival.) Just after Edith and Jennie Grove moved to Great Haywood in early April 1916, Tolkien was posted to the Signalling School at Farnley Park, Otley, in Yorkshire. For perhaps as much as a month, he was taught a combination of old and new methods of communication, such as flag, lamp, and heliograph, employing Morse and other codes. He also became more familiar with the use of field telephones and signal rockets. The logistics of establishing communication stations, employing despatch riders, map reading, and running telephone cables came into it. His training took place in neat and tidy situations, far from the ordered chaos he was to experience on the real battlefront.

G.B. Smith of the T.C.B.S. found that he would be able to make a quick visit, as part of some leave, to see Tolkien and Edith. His train arrived at Great Haywood on Saturday 27 May and he stayed overnight. Afterwards he wrote thanking Tolkien for a "splendid two days". It turned out that his friend would soon be following him to France as, on Friday 2 June, Tolkien received a telegram from Army Headquarters, Cannock Chase, saying that he was to join the British Expeditionary Force in France. Such a telegram was rather like receiving a curt message from the Angel of Death. Tolkien was to report at Folkestone harbour on 5 June, and was granted the usual forty-eight hours' leave. Hastily he and Edith arranged to stay overnight in Birmingham, at the Plough and Harrow Hotel in Edgbaston. This was close by the familiar Oratory, with its friends such as Father Francis. Then, on Sunday 4 June, Edith watched him leave by train from New Street Station, bound for London, and on to the south-east coast. Sitting on the train, Tolkien knew that junior officers were "being killed off, a dozen a minute". He recalled this in an interview many years later, when remembering that departure for war. He added: "Parting from my wife then – we were only just married – it was like a death."[7]

By 6 June, Tolkien had set foot in Calais on the flat coast of northern France. Like all first-timers in the theatre of war his first destination was Étaples (commonly called "Eat-Apples" by the troops or "Tommys"). Here he received the usual short, sharp shock of final training before moving to the front lines.

Tolkien was dismayed that the gear he had bought – carefully selected from the list that Smith had sent him long before – failed to turn up. He hastily had to procure items such as a sleeping bag, camp bed and mattress, and spare boots. After temporary placements he was now, at last, to be with the 11th Battalion of the Lancashire Fusiliers.

He still regretted not being in Smith's 19th battalion, which sometimes however was nearby. Battalions were in theory made up of a thousand men, but the number reduced during battle. Because Britain at this time was strongly regional in character, this tended to be reflected in the battalions fighting in the First World War. The 11th Lancashire Fusiliers was made up of soldiers from a group of northern towns, including Preston, Blackburn, Burnley, Wigan, Oldham, and Bolton. Tolkien felt an affinity with these working men, even though, as an officer, he was forced to keep his distance. He would have keenly noticed their use of "Lanky", a dialect that was widespread, and also popular in entertainment for people outside of those who spoke it naturally.[8] Like all officers, Tolkien had a batman to look after him and take care of his kit, and he remarked in later life that the character of the Hobbit who accompanied Frodo Baggins on his quest to destroy the Ring owed much to his wartime contact with the ordinary "Tommy": "My 'Sam Gamgee' is indeed a reflexion of the English soldier, of the privates and batmen I knew in the 1914 war, and recognized as so far superior to myself."[9]

Three of the T.C.B.S. were now on the Western Front; Christopher Wiseman alone was elsewhere, on the high seas or in harbour. They kept in touch with each other as much as they could. Rob Gilson, who was serving with the Suffolk

Regiment, wrote to Tolkien on 22 June. The talk was of an Allied offensive, a Big Push, at the end of June in the vicinity of Albert, which is on a tributary near the River Somme, and close by the front lines. Gilson had received a note from Tolkien as he returned from a trench working party (he had become something of an expert on trench works). In his reply he confessed:

> I have never felt more forcibly than in the last few weeks, the truth of your words about the oasis of TCBSianism. Life just now is a veritable desert: a fiery one. The TCBS never despised the ordeal and I don't think they underrated it, mine has of late increased in intensity. None the less I am cheerful enough and more grateful than I can say for the breaths of cool fresh air which the various members of the TCBS have given me from time to time.[10]

The rumours turned out to be true (in the event, the attack was postponed by a day), and the Germans had got wind of them, also, and were prepared for an onslaught. The occasion of Tolkien's arrival in France meant, in fact, that he was in position with the 11th Lancashire Fusiliers just in time for one of the greatest battles of the First World War, and one of the costliest in casualties. This was the Battle of the Somme. The opposing front lines ran from the North Sea coast to Switzerland; for their northernmost part they lay north-south before veering eastwards towards Verdun and the German border and then south to the Swiss border. The battle took place in the area where the front lines intersected with the River Somme, on its sluggish journey westward towards the

English Channel. Ironically, the river's name, it is said, derives from a Celtic word meaning "tranquillity".[11]

The battle began in July. When it was over in mid-November, the total Allied gain was about five miles, 300,000 soldiers from both sides killed, and double that figure wounded. Among the enemy injured at the Somme was Corporal Adolf Hitler, who later described the battle as "more like hell than war". The Allies expected it to be a decisive breakthrough instead of the dismal stalemate it turned out to be. The Allies' strategy was to put all their faith in a week-long artillery barrage before their forces advanced. So confident of success was General Haig that troops were ordered to walk slowly towards enemy lines in close waves. Once these were occupied, the idea was that cavalry units would then surge through in pursuit of retreating Germans. Around 1.7 million shells were fired in that relentless barrage. Gilson described the scene in a letter home: "Guns firing at night are beautiful – if they were not so terrible. They have the grandeur of thunderstorms."[12]

Lieutenant Rob Gilson died on 1 July, the first day. He fell just after taking over the command of his battalion in No-Man's Land. As Gilson and his men had awaited the 7.30 a.m. whistle to advance, they heard birds singing, and saw wild flowers in woodland and garden flowers around a small chateau. Gilson was the first of the T.C.B.S. to die (apart from the premature death of Vincent Trought over four years before). He was twenty-two. That first day set the theme of futile slaughter: Gilson was just one of over 19,000 British soldiers who died in the advance. More than 36,000 were injured.[13] Of all the officers employed in battle that day, up to 60 per cent may have died.[14] Tolkien's battalion was not ordered into action in that first advance, being reserved for later. Because Gilson's body was not recovered immediately, he was listed as missing for some time.

Unaware of their friend's death, G.B. Smith and Tolkien met up several times between 6 and 8 July in Bouzincourt, north-west of Albert, where Tolkien was briefly stationed. They found that they were near each other when Smith had a rest period. This was before returning to the front, where he had survived the terrible early days of the battle. According to Humphrey Carpenter, they "met and talked as often as they could, discussing poetry, the war, and the future. Once they walked in a field where poppies still waved in the wind despite the battle that was turning the countryside into a featureless desert of mud". They were anxious for news of Rob Gilson.

In response to his friend's death, G.B. Smith spoke for the others of the T.C.B.S. when he afterwards wrote:

Let us tell quiet stories of kind eyes
    And placid brows where peace and learning sate:
Of misty gardens under evening skies
    Where four would talk of old, with steps sedate.

Let's have no word of all the sweat and blood,
    Of all the noise and strife and dust and smoke
(We who have seen Death surging like a flood,
    Wave upon wave, that leaped and raced and broke).

Or let's sit quietly, we three together,
    Around a wide hearth-fire that's glowing red,
Giving no thought to all the stormy weather
    That flies above the roof-tree overhead.

And he, the fourth, that lies all silently
In some far-distant and untended grave,
Under the shadow of a shattered tree,
Shall leave the company of the hapless brave,

And draw nigh unto us for memory's sake,
Because a look, a word, a deed, a friend,
Are bound with cords that never a man may break,
Unto his heart for ever, until the end.[15]

Tolkien's initial response to the death of Gilson, a year his junior, was different from his later reaction to Smith's — at first, he despaired over their aspirations about the future of the T.C.B.S.[16] But as the surviving members communicated with each other, their encouragement helped his hope to return.

Tolkien's first taste of action took place on the evening of Friday 14 July. As he went into the unknown, he carried the knowledge of Gilson's death two weeks before. What he was to call the "animal horror" of the lines, with their maze of trenches, lay before him. With his battalion he clambered through a mile of communication gullies cut through to the front line. As a signaller he faced a confusion of chaotic wires and dud field-telephones half-buried in the eternal mud. There were bans on many of the signalling options he expected to be available to him, demanding extreme resourcefulness. It often meant falling back on the use of carrier pigeons. He was the battalion signals officer, his responsibility to oversee communications to the brigade command post, which lay a mile and a half behind the lines. Communication was at the centre of battle, affecting the fate of those who fought. In the trenches, sometimes, wherever Tolkien looked, there were corpses waiting to be removed; not peaceful, reclining cadavers, but remains disfigured by shelling. In No-Man's Land, past the trenches, bodies were everywhere, swelling and putrid with decay. The stench defied description. No wonder Tolkien remembered it as "animal horror". The law of the jungle was amplified by machine-efficient slaughter. Then, as summer became autumn, constant, cold rain multiplied the mud into what seemed an ocean, absorbing thousands of shattered or contorted corpses.

The experience of that night was repeated and reinforced many times. His next exposure to the front was just after the death of another friend, Ralph Payton, within weeks of Gilson's. On 22 July, "The Baby", as the T.C.B.S. had called him to distinguish him from his elder brother, died during a night assault. He was leading machine gunners of the 1st Birmingham Battalion on high ground, "High Wood", as it was called, which was strewn with the corpses of horses previously cut down in the only cavalry charge in the Battle of the Somme. Like many, Payton's body was never found. Almost the entire battalion was obliterated in the assault in which he died.

In late September, Tolkien's battalion captured some Germans. He remembered with amusement what happened when he offered a drink of water to a wounded officer. As he accepted the drink, the officer corrected Tolkien on his pronunciation of German! Tolkien was unable to become emotionally distant from the horror. After one of his signallers, Private Sydney Sumner, disappeared during heavy shelling (his body was never found), Tolkien was passed a pleading letter from his distraught wife:

> I have not heard from him for this long time, but we
> have had news from the army chaplain that he has been
> missing since July the 9th. Dear Sir I would not care if I
> only knew how he went. I know that they cannot all be
> saved to come home...[17]

Sydney Sumner had left a one-year-old daughter. Tolkien kept
several of such letters that he had had to answer.

Except for basic, scrawled notes, Tolkien didn't write
stories while he was in the trenches, as some have thought.
"That's all spoof," he rejoined in an interview. "You might
scribble something on the back of an envelope and shove it
in your back pocket but that's all. You couldn't write. This
[pointing to his converted garage] would be an enormous
dugout. You'd be crouching down among flies and filth."[18] It
is likely that he developed stories, themes, and ideas in his
head as he toiled through the catastrophe of the drawn-out
battle. Some of what he experienced was to influence his
future writings, probably in many more ways than we as
readers can be aware, given the complexity and variety of
his sources.

One indication of how memories of modern war haunted
him is in "The Passage of the Marshes" in *The Lord of the Rings*.
Here we read of Sam tripping, as he hurried forward. His
hand sank into the bog. Springing back, he had cried out in
horror that there were dead faces in the water. Gollum had
laughed at his reaction, and explained the name, "the Dead
Marshes". There had been a great battle long ago, in which
men and Elves had fallen in great numbers. For Tolkien,
those long-dead faces staring up from under the water could
include his fallen friends, such as Rob Gilson.

Then, before the Battle of the Somme stalled and ended, Tolkien was taken ill. In the filthy conditions in the trenches, lice were rife. Like many others, he contracted what was called "trench fever", usually a five-day infection. Tolkien's, however, persisted and on the final day of the Battle, 18 November, the decision was made to evacuate him to England. From the constant anxiety of the trenches, and the remorseless rhythm of front-line engagement, and short breaks from it, Tolkien found himself in a military hospital in Birmingham. The giant ward in which he lay was actually the Great Hall of Birmingham University, in the suburb of Selly Oak, requisitioned for war use. It was less than six months since he had bid farewell to Edith at New Street Station, a few miles away. He had come back a man who was changed forever by the trauma of war.

Soon after Tolkien arrived in Birmingham, on 29 November G.B. Smith of the T.C.B.S. was caught in shellfire, and shrapnel entered his thigh and right arm. As one of the walking wounded, he was able to make his own way to the dressing station to wait for an ambulance. He died a few days later as his wounds became gangrenous. The loss of two of his three closest friends – one of them truly a soulmate – was a strong motivation for Tolkien to write down his mythology, to make some sense of their aspirations. He later observed: "A real taste for fairy-stories was wakened by philology on the threshold of manhood, and quickened to full life by war." He was not talking about diminutive fairies among the flowers and little children's stories, but tales that strayed into the dangerous realms of creatures with strange and marvellous powers who fought against terrors and evils and pointed out to men and women the way of courage, virtue, goodness, and self-sacrifice. Tolkien had experienced the full reality of evil and its assault on humanity in war. Now his imagination was alert and strong, and starting to work to turn this reality – if the vision of the T.C.B.S. was correct – into poetry and stories that would help to change the world and reduce its darkness. Gilson and Smith stood behind him in spirit as he did so, and Christopher Wiseman, his fellow survivor, was beside him, though separated by sea, dreaming of what the two of them might do after the war, in keeping with the bright vision of the T.C.B.S. Wiseman had written a long letter to Tolkien in hospital that included the comment: "If you do come out in print you will startle our generation as no one has yet."

But first Tolkien had to recover as best he could from the deep mental scars of his ordeal, his trial by fire and water. Then he would at some stage, he expected, be deemed fit to return to the Western Front, in all likelihood to die. He was merely on an extended respite away from the front lines. Though he would no longer see Gilson or Smith in shattered French towns somewhere near the battle, there was, however, Edith.

7

Recovery, "W", and half a million words

Tolkien was declared unfit for military service, and granted leave for six weeks, the first of many such periods. This initial leave lasted until 12 January 1917. Though his temperature at last had fallen, he was suffering from headaches and leg pains. In fact, through periods of remission, his symptoms would relentlessly recur. He was able to offer limited "home" service (as opposed to "general" – that is, duties including active service) much of the time, and was assigned to the 3rd (Reserve) Battalion of the Lancashire Fusiliers. His own battalion, the 11th, continued to see action in Belgium, near Ypres and in the battle for Passchendaele Ridge. In later action in 1918, the battalion was so greatly depleted by death and injury that its survivors, with others in a similar situation, were formed into a new battalion that April. The new group continued to see fierce action through May, and then was wiped out in battle, except for a small reserve. On 12 August 1918, the battalion was declared to be disbanded.

Had Tolkien returned to action with the 11th Lancashire Fusiliers, his survival would have been highly uncertain. His continuing bouts of illness may have been stress-related, as a result of being traumatized by war. The loss of his parents, and other setbacks of his childhood and youth, had perhaps eroded the natural resilience of his nature, making him particularly vulnerable to the horrors he experienced at the Somme, including the loss of two of his closest friends. In stark contrast, his brother Hilary was able to endure military service throughout the war, receiving only minor wounds in battle. Tolkien could not escape his concerns for those he knew. G.B. Smith's widowed mother corresponded with him regularly. She shared her sorrow at her son's death, and urged Tolkien to help in the publication of his poems. On 6 March 1917, Mrs Smith wrote to Tolkien with the news of the death in battle of her younger son, Roger, leaving her alone. "I cannot believe the terrible thing that has befallen me," she said in her letter. "To lose two such fine sons is indeed crushing."[1] Later that year Tolkien heard of the death of his friend and former member of the T.C.B.S., "Tea-Cake" Barnsley, at Ypres, where Hilary Tolkien was wounded around this time.

Recovering in tranquil Great Haywood weeks after his return from France, Tolkien immediately began seriously shaping and writing the tales that would become "The Silmarillion", putting onto paper a story he referred to as "The Fall of Gondolin". This was part of what he called then *The Book of Lost Tales*. Tolkien explained: "Long before I wrote *The Hobbit* and long before I wrote [*The Lord of the Rings*] I had constructed this world mythology."[2] Perhaps he began with this story, because some of it concerned a battle as terrifying as any he had experienced. The story tells of the invasion of the hidden Elven city of Gondolin, the heroism of its defenders, and the escape of Tuor, Eärendil, and others, who figure importantly in the unfolding stories of what will eventually become Middle-earth.

Two and a half months into the 1916 Battle of the Somme, tanks had been used for the first time, further changing the nature of warfare already dependent on shelling from a variety of heavy guns. It is likely that Tolkien drew upon fresh memories of that battle and its new technology of slaughter in "The Fall of Gondolin". In particular, newly created tanks most likely inspired the technological sorcery of his Satan-figure Melko (to be modified to Melkor, and later named Morgoth) in the destruction of the beautiful Elven city of Gondolin. His forces used terrifying metal dragons that travelled on "iron so cunningly linked that they might flow... around and above all obstacles before them".[3] In 1916 the new weapon of mass destruction, the tank, seemed apocalyptic, as in this contemporary German report:

> The monster approached slowly, hobbling. Moving from side to side, rocking and pitching, but it came nearer. Nothing obstructed it: a supernatural force seemed to drive it onwards. Someone in the trenches cried, "The devil comes," and that word ran down the line like lightning. Suddenly tongues of fire licked out of the armoured shine of the iron caterpillar... the English waves of infantry surged up behind the devil's chariot.[4]

Tolkien intended "The Fall of Gondolin" to be a major tale in "The Silmarillion", but it was never completed on a grand scale. *The Silmarillion* (published in 1977, after Tolkien's death) contains a summary of the story, while in *Unfinished Tales* (1980) there is the first part of a detailed treatment showing, sadly, the promise of what was never achieved. The most complete form of "The Fall of Gondolin" is to be found in *The Book of Lost Tales*, but, unfortunately, this was written therefore early in the development of "The Silmarillion".

These early stories such as "The Fall of Gondolin" (later called "Of Tuor and the Fall of Gondolin") remarkably anticipate many of the main features of stories developed by Tolkien over the next fifty years and more belonging to "The Silmarillion". Many of the magical creatures found in *The Hobbit* and *The Lord of the Rings* are there: orcs, dragons, Balrogs, and the noble Elves. In these familiar books there are numerous references to matters covered by "The Silmarillion": ruins of once-great places, sites of battles long ago, strange and beautiful names from the deep past, and Elven swords made in Gondolin, before its fall, for the Goblin Wars. Hobbits are absent as yet, however. Tolkien was not to invent (or, as he would see it, *discover*) them for many more years, bringing their name into the most distinguished English dictionaries. Besides, these stories concerned the deep past of Middle-earth, whereas Hobbits would inhabit its far distant future.

The stories he created in those war years – such as "The Fall of Gondolin" and a story that soon followed, about the love of Beren and Lúthien Tinúviel – came to him, he felt, as something given, rather than as conscious creation. This sense of givenness and discovery remained with him throughout his life. "The Silmarillion" already belongs in essence to this period even though the developed but abridged version was not published until the seventies. In fact, developments of the mythology, history, and tales of Middle-earth conceived in the First World War are found in unfinished drafts spanning over half a century, with considerable developments and changes in narrative structure. Tolkien also did extensive and incredibly detailed work on his invented languages, tied as they were to his stories, including a "Gnomish" lexicon (at that time "Gnomish" essentially meant "Elvish").

A striking feature of *The Book of Lost Tales* is Tolkien's attempt to put "The Silmarillion" into an accessible storytelling framework. The reader can easily get confused when confronted with invented landscapes, names, languages, and histories, as well as magical creatures never before encountered, such as Balrogs and intelligent giant spiders. *The Book of Lost Tales* concerns a human mariner, Eriol (or Aelfwine, "Elf-friend"), who, by chance, sails to Tol Eressëa, the Lonely Island close by the coast of Valinor, land of the angelic powers. There, in a Warwickshire-like setting, he discovers the Cottage of Lost Play. Here Elves narrate to him the tales of the creation of the world by music, Morgoth's destruction of the light of the Two Trees of Valinor, and other stories of "The Silmarillion". There are significant differences of detail from more final forms of the stories, but they are clearly recognizable.

"The Fall of Gondolin", the earliest composed, is one of four stories key to the future form of "The Silmarillion" that appear in *The Book of Lost Tales,* or were planned by Tolkien to appear but not finished. Each of these feature (or would eventually feature) a human protagonist, though one of these heroes is a "Half-elven" – that is, the offspring of mixed Elf and human parentage. That is Eärendil, who then faces a choice between Elven immortality and joining the lot of "mortal man doomed to die". Such a human protagonist (Túrin Turambar, Beren, Tuor, and Eärendil) provides a point of contact for the reader, for whom tales otherwise told from an Elvish perspective might prove too remote from human interest. One of the striking contrasts between the familiar *The Lord of the Rings* and *The Hobbit* on the one hand and *The Silmarillion* on the other is that the first two are told from a Hobbit perspective, which is effectively that of a human observer. *The Silmarillion* is told from the perspective of the Elves.

One of the many returns of ill health put Tolkien into a sanatorium in Harrogate with a high temperature. While there, Christopher Wiseman was able to visit him and Edith during a spell of leave. On 19 April 1917, Tolkien was back on duty with the 3rd Lancashire Fusiliers, based at Thirtle Bridge Camp, near the coastal town of Withernsea in Holderness on the Humber peninsula, in Yorkshire. Holderness is a low-lying region dotted with copses and small woods, looking more like the Netherlands than England. Much of it was marshland before being drained in medieval times. Tolkien would have encountered one of its inhabitants, in the person of an unscrupulous Friar, in studying Chaucer's "The Summoner's Tale" in *The Canterbury Tales* at Oxford. The tale begins: "Lordynges, ther is in Yorkshire, as I gesse,/A mersshy contree called Holdernesse..."[5] (roughly: Ladies and Gentlemen, there is in Yorkshire, as I believe, a marshy country called Holderness). The Fusiliers were in Holderness to train new recruits and to protect the area from possible German invasion. Zeppelins, in fact, bombed some places such as Hornsea, up the coast, and nearby Kingston upon Hull. Around this time Edith with Jennie Grove left Harrogate, in which she had been staying to be near her husband, finding furnished lodgings in Hornsea. She was thankful for his constant periods of illness, as they kept him from France.

During a temporary period in which Tolkien was placed in charge of an outpost, he was given living quarters for a short while in what may have been a "lonely house near Roos" he mentioned in notes, not far from Withernsea. Edith was able to stay with him here. About this time, Edith helped to inspire the great tale of Lúthien and Beren, his first story of "there and back again" and quest, which he created early on in the development of "The Silmarillion". It tells of the love between the Elves Lúthien the princess and Beren. (As the story develops, Beren is portrayed as human rather than an Elf, and Lúthien renounces her immortality in order to marry him.) Beren has to cut a Silmaril, a magical gem, from the Iron Crown of Morgoth to win Lúthien. The story had such a personal meaning for Tolkien that Lúthien and her lover Beren became pet names for Edith and him, reflecting a very deep emotional association. The birth of the story was tied up with an incident when the two of them had wandered in a small wood near Roos, most likely Dents Garth, beside All Saints (Anglican) Church, south of the village on the Halsham road. There, among "hemlock", she danced and sang to him. Beren, in the story, first encounters Lúthien dancing among hemlock in the woods of a hidden Elven kingdom. Tolkien used "hemlock" as a generic name for similar-looking white-flowered umbellifers, which had varied names such as cow parsley, wild chervil, or Queen Anne's lace.[6] In a letter to his son Christopher in 1972, the year before his death, Tolkien said of Edith: "In those days her hair was raven, her skin clear, her eyes brighter than you have seen them, and she could sing – and dance."[7] On their grave in Wolvercote Cemetery, Oxford, the names Lúthien and Beren are inscribed.

Also around this time Tolkien created another story for *The Book of Lost Tales* – that of Túrin Turambar, developed to some extent from the Finnish story of Kullervo from the *Kalevala,* which he had discovered years before. Christopher Tolkien believes that this story, in an early form, was in existence by the middle of 1917. The tragedy of Túrin, "The Tale of Túrin Turambar", is one of several stories from "The Silmarillion" as it developed in later years that stand independently of the history and mythology of Middle-earth. (That is, they can be enjoyed in the same way as *The Hobbit* and *The Lord of the Rings,* where the history and mythology serves as background, but with alluring references, creating perspective and depths.) In its developed form, the story begins with Húrin, the father of Túrin, who had been captured by Morgoth and bound upon the slopes of Thangorodrim, a giant mountain in the icy north, where he could better see the outworkings of Morgoth's curse or doom upon his family. The curse bedevils the life of Túrin, and other relations, including Túrin's sister, Nienor. Yet the sorrow in Túrin's life comes not only from external causes, though compounded by them, but also because of a "fatal flaw" that is the stuff of tragedy. Túrin's flaw was a mixture of pride and rashness of action. In the tension between internal motive and external malice in Túrin's life, Tolkien explores the problem and complexity of evil. He says that in the tale of Túrin "are revealed most evil works of Morgoth", and that it was "the worst of the works of Morgoth in the ancient world". The story exploits one of Tolkien's early loves. Túrin is a dragon-slayer, and his fight against Glaurung the dragon evokes the heroic deeds of Beowulf and of Sigurd. As a child, Tolkien had discovered the tale of Sigurd and Fáfnir the dragon in Andrew Lang's retelling in *The Red Fairy Book*, published in 1890. Lang was a distinguished anthropologist and versatile writer who collected and retold folk and fairy stories. *The Red Fairy Book* was part of a popular series with various colours in their titles. As an adult, Tolkien read the story of Sigurd and Fáfnir in the *Poetic Edda*, and eventually retold it.

A fourth of the major tales of what was to become "The Silmarillion" does not figure as such in *The Book of Lost Tales,* which was written during that intensely productive period of the later war years and convalescence. This was "The Tale of Eärendil", which was his earliest inspiration, as we saw. It only existed as complex summaries, and various outlines that often conflicted with each other. There were, however, a number of poems Tolkien had written on Eärendil, and part of the story was built into another. Unfortunately, the tale of Eärendil cannot be reconstructed from Tolkien's unfinished work in as great detail as the tales of Beren and Lúthien, and of Túrin Turambar.

Commenting on the fertility of his imagination, Tolkien remarked in an interview: "My stories seem to germinate like a snowflake around a piece of dust." The richness and scale of Tolkien's invention at this time also applies to this image – it is rather like a fall of snowflakes!

As 1917 progressed, Tolkien continued to have bouts of illness. While he was based at Thirtle Bridge with the Humber Garrison, Edith with Jennie Grove remained lodging in Hornsea. By this time Edith was expecting their first child. In August, Tolkien was admitted with a fever to "Brooklands", in Cottingham Road, Hull. This was an officers' hospital. The high temperature continued for six weeks. At Brooklands he enjoyed the company, including a patient who was a friend from the Lancashire Fusiliers. He also appreciated visits from nuns from a house of the Sisters of Mercy in Hull. One, Mother Mary Michael, became a friend with whom he would correspond throughout his life. Tolkien also found his stay very productive for his writing. While he was in the hospital, on the night of Tuesday 25 September Zeppelins attacked Hull, dropping sixteen bombs but causing little damage.

Edith became frustrated with the difficult journey to Hull from Hornsea to visit her husband, especially as the pregnancy progressed. She was not able to visit very often. Also, with the increasing restrictions of the pregnancy, she and Jennie Grove grew increasingly discontented with the miserable lodgings. As the expected birth date drew closer, they decided to go to Cheltenham for Edith to have the child. The city had good associations; her mother, Frances, had sought refuge there for her birth, and her years there staying with Uncle and Aunt Jessop were a relief from living in a boarding house. So it was that Edith gave birth to a son on Friday 16 November 1917, at Cheltenham's Royal Nursing Home. While Edith suffered a difficult labour, with serious threat to both mother and child, Tolkien, still not fully recovered, was forced to remain in Hull to attend another medical board. This deemed him fit for all duties at Thirtle Bridge, though not fit for general service for two months. It was not until a week had passed that he was able to see Edith. She was then recovering, and Father Francis (after whom the baby was named) caught the train from Birmingham to baptize John Francis Reuel Tolkien. All Tolkien's children were to carry the name "Reuel", as he did himself – in Hebrew, it meant "friend of God". The baby's godparents were Hilary Tolkien and Mary Incledon, Tolkien's cousin. To pay for Edith's stay in hospital (there was no National Health Service in those days) Tolkien sold the remaining shares in South African mines bequeathed by his late father.

After the christening, Edith, with the faithful Jennie Grove, brought baby John to Roos (near where she had danced for Tolkien in the small wood). Here she was much nearer to her husband, who had just been promoted to full Lieutenant. Months passed in limited military service, and Tolkien persevered with writing and revising *The Book of Lost Tales.* In June 1918, there was unwelcome news: a medical board declared Tolkien fit for "general service" – that is, service that could include a posting to France. Shortly afterwards, he was ordered once again to Cannock Chase, in Staffordshire, to the familiar Rugeley Camp, near Penkridge. Edith and baby John, along with Jennie Grove, moved to an isolated cottage called Gipsy Green, which was quite near the training camp.

Gipsy Green was a happy place for Edith. Tolkien sketched a number of tiny vignettes of domestic life: Edith tending her hair, washing with huge splashes at a basin, playing her beloved piano, and carrying the infant. There too is a uniformed Tolkien cycling away to the camp, John's pram, the baby in his cot, cats dancing, a passing tractor, and much more. An accomplished sketch of Gipsy Green evokes Tolkien's much later creation of Tom Bombadil's cottage in *The Lord of the Rings,* especially when compared with a much later sketch of another somewhat similar cottage he liked, the New Lodge at Stonyhurst College, Lancashire, which seems to take the allusion to Tom Bombadil's cottage further.[8] In the sketches both have prominent chimneys, with a cottage garden bursting with life in the foreground.

In the case of the drawing of New Lodge, bean rows are strongly in evidence. In Tom Bombadil's cottage, in *The Lord of the Rings*, Frodo Baggins sees Tom's garden through an eastern window. There his view was captured by a line of beans on high poles, with their red flowers distinctive, as in the sketch of New Lodge.

With the encouragement of Christopher Wiseman, since the death of G.B. Smith in battle Tolkien had been working on and off to edit an edition of Smith's poems for publication. He enlisted the help of his former English teacher at King Edward's School. R.W. Reynolds not only had connections in London literary circles (including children's author E. Nesbit), but his advice was also welcome. In June or July 1918, *A Spring Harvest,* by Geoffrey Bache Smith, was published by Erskine MacDonald, with a brief note of introduction by J.R.R. Tolkien. It contained fifty-one of Smith's poems composed between 1910 and his death in 1916.

With the young officer's health problems persisting, later that year, on 4 September, Tolkien was declared 100 per cent disabled, and unfit for any service category for two months. As a result he was sent to the Savoy Convalescent Hospital in Blackpool for some time. Edith had decided before this, rather firmly, not to follow her husband's constant moves but to remain in the stability of Gipsy Green with baby John, and Jennie Grove. It had taken her a while to get over the difficult birth, and she wasn't ready to return to a nomadic life. By the beginning of October, the War Office finally authorized Tolkien for "sedentary" employment. Less than two weeks later he was granted a month's leave.

Taking the opportunity given by this leave, Tolkien turned his sights on Oxford. Rumours of peace were in the air.

By the end of October, he had travelled there, seeking out the prospects of academic work. He found that they were not good. When he called on his old tutor in Old Icelandic, however, things began to change. William Craigie could offer him a place on the staff of the New English Dictionary (now known as the Oxford English Dictionary) as an assistant lexicographer, working under him. The massive dictionary was still being compiled. When the war ended, a few days later on 11 November, Tolkien obtained permission from the army to be stationed at Oxford until demobilization. This, he said, was "for the purposes of completing his education".[9] Working on the dictionary would prove to be one of the best ways to extend his learning as a philologist, and to develop the skills required for his unique approach to creating the world and mythology of Middle-earth. In fact, Tolkien has been described as a "philological writer", a label that applies to both his academic and fictional writings.[10] In later years Tolkien confessed that working on the Oxford English Dictionary, he "learned more in those two years than in any other equal period of my life".[11]

What did Tolkien learn from his work on the most ambitious dictionary ever attempted? It had its beginnings in 1857 in a quest to collect unregistered English words, which developed into a project of a dictionary to collect all English words, well over half a million of them. Head of the project was Herbert Coleridge, the brilliant grandson of poet Samuel Taylor Coleridge, whose life was cut short at thirty by tuberculosis. The full dictionary was not completely published in many volumes until 1928. Since then it has constantly been revised, a task made more effective with the creation of an online edition, made freely available through local libraries in the United Kingdom, and through paid subscription worldwide.

In *The Ring of Words: Tolkien and the Oxford English Dictionary,* Peter Gilliver, Jeremy Marshall, and Edmund Weiner reflect upon what Tolkien learned. They are lexicographers themselves, working on the revision of the Dictionary, sharing his fascination with words. One important facet of his experience, they believe, was becoming "intimately familiar" with the processes of creating the Dictionary. He got to know "the ways of thinking which lexicographers need in order to discover and record the history of words... he was to draw on this philological expertise throughout his academic career".[12] A second facet of his experience was its focus upon individual words, which always stimulated Tolkien's rich imagination. "In describing his own creative processes, Tolkien often comments on how the contemplation of an individual word can be the starting point for an adventure in imagination... Could it be that his work on the Dictionary caused this passion [for words] to develop in a unique way?"[13]

The unexpected luck (or, as Tolkien would have seen it, act of providence) in gaining this desirable job marked a turnabout in his health. For one thing, it enabled him to take control of his life, rather than having to follow the winds of military decisions. He immediately sought out lodgings in Oxford for the family, finding a suitable place a few doors up from his old digs in St John Street. Before the end of November, he and Edith, baby John, and Jennie Grove were settling into rooms at number 50. Their new home so close to his student digs was a poignant link to his friend Colin Cullis, with whom he had shared the accommodation four years before. In the post-war pandemic of flu that killed so many millions, Cullis, who suffered poor health, succumbed.

In early January 1919, Tolkien began a workday ritual of setting off for the offices of the Oxford English Dictionary. It was a pleasant walk from St John Street onto St Giles, then past the Martyrs' Memorial and along Broad Street, to the Old Ashmolean building just before the Sheldonian Theatre. He retraced his steps for lunch at home. In a cavernous room, editors and their teams of assistants sat around desks with bookcases nearby crammed with reference books. The high ceiling was supported by rows of classical columns. There, guided by Henry Bradley, Tolkien worked on various words beginning with "W", among other tasks that exploited his formidable knowledge of Old and Middle English as well as related languages. In addition to roots and forms of words, and definitions, Dictionary entries traced the development of their meaning throughout the history of the English language with the help of carefully chosen illustrative quotations. Tolkien's entry on the word "wan", for instance, contains quotations from many sources, including *Beowulf,* Chaucer's *The Knight's Tale,* and Malory's *Le Morte d'Arthur.* Some of the many other "W" entries Tolkien worked on were waggle, waistcoat, wallop, walrus, wampum, wanderer, wariangle, warlock, wasp, water, winter, and wold.

An indication of Tolkien's exceptional gifts, in which he stood out even among his fellow lexicographers on the Oxford English Dictionary, is that over his lifetime he was to add some words to the English language, and was also to reintroduce forgotten English words, at times with a new twist. On occasions, he may have coined a word that, unknown to him, had been used long before in an obscure setting or with a different meaning. (This happened with J.K. Rowling when she coined the term "Muggle".) Not only does the OED carry the fruit of Tolkien's labour in the "W" section, but it also today has entries on some of the words that sprang from his creativity both in his scholarship and in his fiction. Tolkien coined words from scratch such as "Hobbit", "sub-creation" and "sub-creator", "eucatastrophe" ("the sudden happy turn in a story which pierces you with a joy that brings tears"[14]), "warg" (evil wolf), "Wilderland", "legendarium", "mithril" (light but immensely hard metal), and the sinister "Unlight" and revived others like "attercop" (venomous spider), "eleventy", "Afterlithe" (July), and "orc". As a result of Tolkien's way of seeing the world, others have coined the new words "Tolkienian" (also "Tolkinian") and "Tolkienesque", in the style of "Shakespearian" and "Kafkaesque".

Tolkien's labours on the Dictionary did not yield a full income, encouraging him to take a second job tutoring for the university. The students would come in small groups to his home in St John Street for tutorage. As Edith was there, Tolkien was a popular choice for the women's colleges such as Lady Margaret Hall, St Hilda's, Somerville, and St Hugh's, as there was no need to provide a chaperone. Thus he was soon tutoring a number of women in Old English. This was a period following major struggles for emancipation when it began to get easier for women at Oxford. Women over thirty achieved the right to vote in 1918, and would become on a par with men in 1928. In fact, in May 1920 Oxford granted women full membership of the university. Almost all degrees were now open to them, the exceptions at that time being degrees and doctorates in Divinity.

As Tolkien's income increased, the family were able to move late in the summer vacation of 1919 to larger accommodation nearby on the corner of Alfred Street and St Giles. Not only did this mean that Edith could bring her beloved piano out of storage, but that she could also hire a local housemaid–cook to help her.

During his Dictionary work and tutoring, Tolkien was busy reworking and revising *The Book of Lost Tales*. He was also hard at work on an ambitious glossary of Middle English words, to be used with Kenneth Sisam's *Fourteenth Century Verse & Prose,* and commissioned by Oxford University Press. (The glossary was published in 1922 as a separate volume, and also that year bundled in with a new edition of Sisam's collection.) The New Zealander Kenneth Sisam had been popular as Tolkien's tutor when an undergraduate, and was now connected to the Oxford University Press. The glossary contained more than 4,500 entries and close on 7,000 definitions, a colossal undertaking. Tolkien also found time to attend Essay Club meetings at his old college, Exeter. On 10 March 1920, instead of an expected essay, he bravely read out a shortened version of his story "The Fall of Gondolin", the first public exposure of his private mythology. In attendance were students Nevill Coghill and H.V.D. Dyson, who were to become friends and fellow members of the Inklings in the thirties. It was received with great enjoyment. The club minutes read:

> As a discovery of a new mythological background Mr
> Tolkien's matter was exceedingly illuminating and
> marked him out as a staunch follower of tradition,
> a treatment indeed in the manner of such typical

> Romantics as William Morris, George Macdonald,
> de la Motte-Fouque etc.... The battle of the
> contending forces of good and evil as represented
> by the Gondothlim and the followers of Melko was
> very graphically and astonishingly told, combined
> with a wealth of attendance to detail interesting in
> extreme....[15]

By the end of May 1920, Tolkien had stopped working for the Dictionary. He was as busy as ever, including the task of applying for a senior position – a readership in English Language – at Leeds University. Kenneth Sisam, no doubt impressed by his work on the Middle English glossary, told him of the vacancy. Unlike some, Tolkien had no prejudices against northern counties. He had served in the trenches with the Lancashire Fusiliers, and had an enormous respect for Joseph Wright, the linguistic genius from Yorkshire who had previously inspired him as an undergraduate with Comparative Philology and had done extensive studies of English dialect and an ancient language Tolkien loved, Gothic. He placed his hopes on the Leeds post. This is not to say that he had no niggling doubts about leaving Oxford. For one thing, Edith was settled in the Alfred Street house. For another, Tolkien had a strong emotional attachment to the place. His health had been restored as he threw himself into his work on the Dictionary, his tutoring in Old English, and his inspired preparation of a Middle English glossary to help students of fourteenth-century literature. Throughout the sheer hard work these tasks entailed, his imagination had still soared as he developed the languages, world, history, and legends of what was to become Middle-earth.

8

Leeds and dragons

Leeds University lacked the bright, ancient splendour of Oxford. The sooty air from its manufacturing industry made its mock Gothic Victorian buildings grimy. A short walk from its Great Hall there were rows of terraced houses, within one of which the English Department was housed. Today, the large modern buildings making up the frontage of the university hide the Great Hall and other main buildings of the original institution, which reveal that smaller colleges had existed here – most recently the Yorkshire College – before the university's formation in 1904, sixteen years before Tolkien's arrival. The English Department location of the time has long been demolished.

Tolkien was soon made to feel at home. The English Department was rapidly expanding under Professor George S. Gordon, who had come from Oxford University for this purpose. He extended a free hand to Tolkien to form a School of English Philology within the English Department, in which literary and linguistic interests would work together. Gordon introduced the Oxford English School syllabus, in which students could choose between some specialist courses in medieval English language and literature, and some in more modern literature. This task was a challenge to inspire a person of Tolkien's precocious gifts. Though the Yorkshire students at first seemed dull and stodgy, he soon found them hard-working and quick to make progress. Eventually, from only a small proportion taking specialist courses involving English language, a much larger number were attracted.

Before Tolkien began teaching in his new position at Leeds, the family had taken a holiday cottage on the North Wales coast at Llanbedrog for part of the long summer vacation. (Much of the vacation was taken up for Tolkien by marking school examination papers for extra income to pay medical bills, and similar.) The resort combined Tolkien's love of the sea and some exposure to the Welsh language. What was not pleasant were the spiders that fell from the ceiling onto Edith's bed. She was fairly well advanced in pregnancy at the time, and did not appreciate such shocks. Edith was carrying their second son, Michael, and she and Tolkien would tell him in later years that his fear of spiders sprang from Edith's experience. As usual, Tolkien painted and sketched on holiday, and at Llanbedrog he composed a couple of impressions of the Irish Sea coast.

Edith remained in Alfred Street with John, and Jennie Grove, while Tolkien began his first term as Reader in English and started to look around for suitable accommodation for his growing family. At weekends he became familiar with the railway route from Leeds to Oxford. In October 1920 the family celebrated the successful birth of Michael Hilary Reuel Tolkien. Then Christmas that year, which was spent in Oxford, saw the beginning of Tolkien's Father Christmas letters, annual letters he wrote and illustrated for his children until 1943. These were eventually collected and published after his death. Tolkien was very much a family man.

It was not until March the following year that Tolkien found accommodation for the family in Leeds. For a few months they rented 5 Holly Bank, a house owned by Miss Moseley, a niece of Cardinal Newman. Then they moved to 11 St Mark's Terrace, near the university. Neither house exists today. Because of city pollution, spots of soot would fall on baby Michael if he was placed outside in his pram for a period of time. Tolkien had already discovered that he had to change his shirt collar (detachable) three times a day.

With the move to Leeds, Jennie Grove returned to Birmingham. She remained a much-loved "grandmother" figure to the growing children. After being at St Mark's Terrace for some time, Edith took on another maid. Some months later their house was turned over by organized burglars. Among family items stolen were Edith's finest coat and her engagement ring. Neither was recovered. The thieves showed no interest in Tolkien's books. It turned out that the maid was a member of the gang of burglars. As a result of this experience, when Bilbo Baggins was termed a "burglar" in *The Hobbit,* the word had a special meaning for Tolkien, and to his children to whom he first told the story!

At Leeds University Tolkien continued to flourish, combining his academic activities with his creations for "The Silmarillion". His glossary for the compilation of extracts from Middle English by Kenneth Sisam finally was complete, published as *A Middle English Vocabulary* by Oxford University Press. In 1922 a young Canadian lecturer, Eric Valentine Gordon, joined the university English Department. Tolkien already knew the former Rhodes Scholar, having tutored him at Oxford. They were soon collaborating on an ambitious edition of *Sir Gawain and the Green Knight*, published in 1925. This presentation of the text of what Tolkien regarded as the finest of all the English medieval romances helped to stimulate study of this work. The edition also contains a major glossary. Tolkien was a perfectionist, working meticulously, and was to be constantly late with publishers' deadlines, sometimes never producing the required manuscript at all. In contrast, Gordon was efficient without being slow, and Tolkien had a job keeping up with him (he provided the edited text and glossary, and Gordon the notes). In fact, Tolkien described his colleague as "an industrious little devil". Gordon and Tolkien also formed the Viking Club for their students – which included translating nursery rhymes into Anglo-Saxon, making comic songs, and getting the students to enjoy rousing drinking songs in Old Norse. Tolkien even made at least one crossword puzzle in Old English to draw in his students. The Club was undoubtedly popular with them: soon a higher proportion were taking the language option than in the Oxford English School.

During this period Tolkien worked on a verse translation of the great Old English poem *Beowulf,* and also a complete prose translation, as yet still lying unpublished in the Bodleian Library special collection. His verse translations display his remarkable mastery of the alliterative form of poetry, which he also was to use in his unfinished poetic version of a tale from "The Silmarillion", that of Túrin Turambar (where, at one stage, he called the typescript "The Golden Dragon"). In this ancient form of verse, alliteration is the guiding principle – Tolkien once called it "chiming" rather than "rhyming". (Alliteration in general employs the reoccurrence of the same initial sound in words that are in close succession; in Old English and similar languages the verse form is quite complex.) C.S. Lewis once illustrated alliteration for his students at Oxford:

We were talking of dragons, Tolkien and I
In a Berkshire bar. The big workman
Who sat silent and sucked his pipe
All the evening, from his empty mug
With gleaming eye glanced towards us;
"I seen 'em myself", he said fiercely.[1]

Tolkien had a remarkable ear for the vocal beauty of the Old English and Middle English originals, a beauty that he could transpose into modern English. His translations were far from wooden renderings, yet remained accurate.

Around this time Tolkien began to tell stories to young John when he was unable to sleep, a habit of storytelling that would extend to his other children as they grew, which ultimately was to lead to the creation of *The Hobbit*. One he told to John was about a boy with red hair called Carrots who has a number of adventures after climbing into a cuckoo clock.

Edith had found home life at Leeds congenial. She was relaxing into a more settled existence after the often nomadic existence of many earlier years, including the period of living in lodgings in Edgbaston and moving to Cheltenham after Father Francis's ultimatum. It was difficult to make Tolkien's income stretch to all their needs, even when supplemented by his marking of exam papers in the summer vacations. They were saving hard to buy a house rather than endure the restrictions of rented property. Edith carefully recorded their income and outgoings. She enjoyed the friendly university atmosphere, and got to know wives of Tolkien's colleagues. They did on occasions get to the Yorkshire coast for holidays.

Filey did not strike the right note as a choice of holiday resort. Tolkien expressed dislike of the place, and the state of the beach. Nevertheless this small coastal town on a wide bay played a significant part in the Tolkien family history. Filey lies south of Whitby, which Tolkien had visited in his youth in the summer of 1910. This stretch of the north-eastern coast is rich in the history of early Christianity. At Whitby, Tolkien would have come across the name of St Hilda, and her protégé, Caedmon, whose verse greatly influenced early English poetry, but only a few lines of which have survived. Filey is less than thirty miles from Whitby. When in Whitby, Tolkien had elaborately sketched its harbour. Filey (the town, not the area) was much less to his taste. He described it as "a very nasty little suburban seaside resort". Yet he wrote poems on it in which the area becomes "Bimble Bay". The town, even with his negative perception of it, could not have spoiled Filey's extensive bay, which has eroded mud cliffs in places, and a long strand. There is a wide promenade that gently slopes down to the beach. The family thought enough of it to return there for another holiday, three years later, in 1925, which inspired a bedtime story that became Tolkien's first written children's story. This was *Roverandom*.

During that three-week holiday, the Tolkien family stayed in a cottage on a low cliff. Because of the clear view over the sea that this gave, they were able to see a remarkable full moonrise above the wide horizon. The shining of its light on the ocean seemed like a silver path to the shore. This was an important seed for the story that Tolkien was to tell his children. The immediate impetus for it, however, was that four-year-old Michael Tolkien lost his little lead dog on the beach. It was painted black and white, and he was totally attached to it. For two days they searched in vain for it among the pebbles. Then, one night, there was a terrific storm.

Being high on the cliff, they all felt particularly vulnerable as the winds blasted. They feared that the roof might be torn off the cottage. To calm the boys' fears, he told them the story that became *Roverandom*. It also was created in sympathy for Michael's loss of his toy dog, which was not there to comfort him. Tolkien sat up all night because of the fear of damage to the cottage from the storm.

The story was about a real dog, Rover, who is turned into a toy by a Wizard. When dropped on the beach by a small boy, the toy is transported to the moon along the path of light the moon makes when it shines over the sea. The Man in the Moon renames him Roverandom and gives him wings. Roverandom sets out on a series of adventures, encountering the Great White Dragon and other moon fauna such as giant spiders and dragon-moths. Finally, back on Earth, Roverandom travels under the sea inside Uim, oldest of the whales, to ask the Wizard who changed him into a toy to undo the spell. Not immediately, but some time afterwards, the story was written down and illustrated by Tolkien, but not published until 1998, over seventy years after that seaside holiday. Writing down the story may have eased the way for a similar process with the adventures of Bilbo Baggins, which came later, where the tale was first told by Tolkien to his children and then put on paper, as well as illustrated.[2] Certainly, *The Hobbit* is told with engaging flair, unlike the earlier Roverandom story, which was never polished by Tolkien for publication. Also, when *The Hobbit* was told, the children were older, and the story was scaled accordingly. They were more critical by then.

The day after the storm, the family surveyed its wake. The wild tide had swept debris right onto the promenade, destroying beach huts. Later that holiday, they had a memorable walk miles down the coast to Flamborough Head, whose chalky cliffs jut out into the sea, and provide a base for a large lighthouse erected in the nineteenth century to lessen the appalling loss of life from frequent shipwrecks. The purpose of their long trek was to view a German submarine wrecked near Flamborough Head during the war.

"Tales and Songs of Bimble Bay" is a collection of poems partly inspired by Filey and its bay. Humphrey Carpenter comments: "One, suggested by his feelings about Filey, complains of the sordid noisy character of modern urban life. Another, 'The Dragon's Visit', describes the ravages of a dragon who arrives at Bimble Bay and encounters 'Miss Biggins'. A third, 'Glip', tells of a strange slimy creature who lives beneath the floor of a cave and his pale luminous eyes. All," suggests Carpenter, "are glimpses of important things to come."[3] There are hints of the topography of 1920s Filey in the poems, with its cliffs, and caves of wet stones ("wet walls of shining grey"), its long shore, and an unflattering picture of rubbish left by trippers being churned by the waves. A disgruntled portrait of the town gives a vivid impression of its main street arising steeply from the seafront, and its shops, library, houses, motor garages, and traffic noise, a town that is very much adapted to the tastes of holiday makers, many of whom arrive by train and charabanc.

In the summer vacation of 1923, while at Leeds, the Tolkien family visited his brother, Hilary, who had bought a market garden and plum and apple orchard close to Evesham (associated for Tolkien with his Suffield ancestors, and thus his long-lost mother Mabel). There was much to do and the visitors threw in any help that they could provide. John and Michael were delighted when their father and Uncle Hilary flew giant kites. It may have been at this time that Tolkien visited his aunt Jane Neave, on a farm about fifteen miles north in Dormston, near Inkberrow. By 1923 she had moved from Phoenix Farm in Nottinghamshire to work here. The farm she had taken on was called "Bag End" by local people, and marked thus on old maps of the area. Bag End was, in Tolkien's words, "an old tumbledown manor house at the end of an untidy lane that led nowhere else".[4] Like the source of Hobbiton – that is, Sarehole at the end of the nineteenth century – Bag End in Dormston belonged in the original Shire, in Worcestershire.

In the spring of 1924 the family moved to a huge house then on the northern fringe of the city. Number 2 Darnley Road, West Park, had three storeys, with spacious fields nearby for walking. Here Edith had more room for the growing family, though she was disappointed to be pregnant again, and then, in the autumn when Christopher was born, that it was another boy.[5] Christopher was named after his father's T.C.B.S. friend Christopher Wiseman.

In October 1924 Tolkien began his appointment to the Chair of English Language at Leeds University, aged thirty-two, which was remarkably young for a professorship. Professor Tom Shippey was throughout the 1980s and beyond holder of Tolkien's Chair at Leeds. Although many years had passed since Tolkien was there, his mark was still on the English syllabus. He commented: "Tolkien's professional career in the 1920s was... extremely successful. With the encouragement of his head of department at Leeds, George S. Gordon, he built up the language side of the English department until it rivalled literature in popularity with undergraduates...." Shippey adds that after he returned to

Oxford in 1925, "Tolkien's academic career in some respects began to lose impetus."[6] This was not to say that he published no more contributions to philology and English Studies that were hugely significant, argued Shippey, but that his scholarly work tended thereafter to feed more and more into his fiction. In other words (if I've got Shippey correct) his fiction was to become, for him, the main place in which to make scholarly exploration in his chosen area of philology. He was following, perhaps, in the footprints of the great Jacob Grimm, whose work in language turned him to the collection of folk and fairy tales. The mystery of language itself bedazzled Tolkien, just as C.S. Lewis was enchanted by the power of the human (and divine) imagination. This turning of great learning to fiction made possible a unique work like *The Lord of the Rings,* and the superb though unfinished tales of "The Silmarillion" like those of Beren and Lúthien, and of Túrin Turambar.

Tolkien's thoughts turned once again to Oxford. He was now an external examiner there, and also had constant contact with Oxford University Press, and his former tutor there, Kenneth Sisam. Early in 1925 he heard that the Professorship of Anglo-Saxon was to fall vacant, and decided to apply, though he knew the competition would be fierce.

9

Oxford and C. S. Lewis

It was in October 1925 that Tolkien was appointed Rawlinson and Bosworth Professor of Anglo-Saxon at Oxford. His former tutor Kenneth Sisam was one of those who had been in the running for the post. Life was not so simple that he could leave Leeds and move his family to Oxford at this time. It had not been long since he had been elected to the Chair by a vote of four votes to three on 21 July. Tolkien then had to inform Leeds of his plans. Both his old and new employers were able to schedule an arrangement whereby he taught at Leeds and Oxford during the Michaelmas (autumn) term. He did not actually vacate his Chair at Leeds until 31 December 1925, so continued living in north Leeds, in Darnley Road, with Edith and the rest of the family, and lecturing in Oxford on Fridays and Saturdays as part of his professorial duties. That term, his subjects in Oxford were extracts from the philologist Henry Sweet's standard primer, *An Anglo-Saxon Reader in Prose and Verse*, and the text of *Beowulf*. He also supervised postgraduate students working on their B.Litt. theses. One was on the subject of "England and the English in the Icelandic Saga". He was required to be at committee meetings at both universities throughout this period. Tolkien was held in affection by his students at Leeds, who made a collection for his photographic portrait to hang in the Department of English.

According to custom he was, at the same time as becoming a professor, assigned a fellowship with one of the Oxford colleges, in his case Pembroke. At this time there were only three Chairs in the school: Tolkien's Chair for Anglo-Saxon, which he held from 1925 to 1945, and two Chairs specifically linked with Merton College, one for literature (now held by the omnicompetent George S. Gordon, who had come south from Leeds three years before) and one for language and literature. Tolkien was to be Merton Professor of Language and Literature from 1945 until his retirement in 1959. His academic work continued to be intimately related to his construction of the languages, peoples, and history of the three Ages of Middle-earth, though the second increasingly became his main focus. As a result his academic publications would become rarer, but always significant. However, he invariably would do more than was required in his lecturing and supervision of students.

J.I.M. Stewart was an academic, novelist and famous crime writer (under the pseudonym of Michael Innis). In his "campus novel" *Memorial Service,* his fictional portrayal of Tolkien in the person of Oxford Professor of Anglo-Saxon, J.B. Timbermill, is brilliantly accurate about growing perceptions of his real-life counterpart. There were murmurs and rumours about Timbermill's lack of productivity, except when it came to writing *The Magic Quest*:

"A sad case," [the Regius Professor] concluded
unexpectedly.

"Timbermill's, you mean?"

"Yes, indeed. A notable scholar, it seems.
Unchallenged in his field. But he ran off the rails
somehow, and produced a long mad book – a kind of
apocalyptic romance."[1]

As professorships were university-wide and not college
appointments, the responsibilities were quite varied: Tolkien
was required to give a quota of open lectures to undergraduates
(around thirty-five a year, though Tolkien did many more
than this), to teach the relatively few graduate students,
and, primarily, to advance his subject area, particularly by
publication. Tolkien in fact published modestly in his subject,
choosing to invest his knowledge in generations of students
and graduates, whom he always treated courteously and
conscientiously. The other investment of his knowledge
would increasingly be in the world of Middle-earth he was
creating (or "sub-creating", to use his invented term).

In the year Tolkien took up the Chair of Anglo-Saxon,
the poet W.H. Auden came to Oxford as an undergraduate.
There Auden developed a particular liking for Old English
literature. Like Tolkien, Auden had a deep interest in
northern mythology, and he was influenced by the young
professor while at Oxford. He also had grown up in
Birmingham. In later years Tolkien was greatly encouraged
by Auden's enthusiasm for *The Lord of the Rings*. The poet
wrote on the quest hero in Tolkien's work, corresponded
about and discussed with him the meaning of his work, and
counteracted through reviews some of the negative criticism

of the trilogy. In Humphrey Carpenter's biography of Auden (1981) there is a photograph from the 1940s of the poet fully absorbed in reading *The Hobbit*.

Tolkien had a strong theatrical bent, as we have seen. He had enjoyed acting as Mrs Malaprop in the King Edward's School production of Sheridan's *The Rivals* in 1911, in which several of his T.C.B.S. friends had participated. In later years he would be surprised at the dramatic power of his readings from his poetry and *The Lord of the Rings*, captured on a friend's early-model tape recorder. As a lecturer he quickly discovered the effectiveness of opening a lecture with reading *Beowulf* aloud. This early English poem, as was the style of the period, began with *Hwaet*, "Listen!" To novice undergraduates it sounded remarkably like "Quiet!" In a lecture many years later, Auden looked back to the effect that Tolkien had had on him:

> I remember [a lecture] I attended, delivered by Professor Tolkien. I do not remember a single word he said but at a certain point he recited, and magnificently, a long passage of *Beowulf*. I was spellbound. This poetry, I knew was going to be my dish. I became willing, therefore, to work at Anglo-Saxon because, unless I did, I should never be able to read this poetry. I learned enough to read it, however sloppily, and Anglo-Saxon and Middle English poetry have been one of my strongest, most lasting influences.[2]

Auden also spoke about the impact of hearing Tolkien recite from *Beowulf* in a letter he wrote to him in later life: "I don't think I have ever told you what an unforgettable experience it was for me as an undergraduate, hearing you recite *Beowulf*. The voice was the voice of Gandalf."[3] Auden was an atheist in the 1920s. In later years he acknowledged the influential Danish thinker Søren Kierkegaard, Charles Williams (who became a member of the Inklings in the Second World War years), and C.S. Lewis, all of whom, he said, "guided me back to belief",[4] and would privately tell the Catholic Tolkien that the title poem in his book *Homage to Clio* (1960) was a homage to the Virgin Mary.[5]

J.I.M. Stewart was also, like Auden, a student of Tolkien's in those early days. Stewart remarked, "He could turn a lecture room into a mead hall in which he was the bard and we were the feasting listening guests."

A Canadian postgraduate also heard Tolkien lecture in these early days, and remembered:

> He came in lightly and gracefully, I always remember that, his gown flowing, his fair hair shining, and he read *Beowulf* aloud.... The terrors and the dangers that he recounted – how I do not know – made our hair stand on end. He read like no one else I have ever heard. The lecture room was crowded – it was in the Examination Halls, and he was a young man then, for his position, long before *The Hobbit* or the Trilogy were to make him famous. I took a seminar from him also, on Gothic. He was a great teacher, and delightful, courteous, ever so kindly.[6]

In complete contrast, Tolkien was to gain a reputation as one of the university's worst lecturers. Twenty years later, after the Second World War, the novelist Kingsley Amis and poet Philip Larkin in their student days made fun of his impenetrable speech. Amis declared him "incoherent and often inaudible".[7] He also remembered that Tolkien "spoke unclearly and slurred the important words, and then he'd write them on the blackboard but keep standing between them and us, then wipe them off before he turned around".[8] This new generation of writers, as represented by Kingsley Amis and Larkin, reacted against the dominance of Old and Middle English in the Oxford syllabus, and thought that it didn't help them to have the impediment of Tolkien!

In later years, Kingsley Amis began to appreciate the syllabus that Tolkien had created. In his *Memoirs*, he writes:

> And yet since those [Oxford] days, since I left the academic profession some fifteen years later, since my own works began to be studied at universities alongside those of other living writers, and to be written upon by those who taught at such places – well, I have become pretty sure that I and others had things the wrong way round, that philology, however laborious, is a valid subject of academic study, and those post-Chaucerian poems and plays and novels we turned to with such relief are not. They are to be approached instead in the spirit of self-cultivation and entertainment. Ask yourself whether our literature has improved or declined since it began to be studied as university subject. Start with English poetry.[9]

But this was the future. Early in January 1926, after his laborious term the previous year teaching at both universities, Tolkien moved his family from Leeds to 22 Northmoor Road, not far north of Oxford's city centre. From here he found it easy to commute to Pembroke College, a little further south of Carfax, named after the tower of the ancient church of St Martin. According to his children John and Priscilla, "He became a familiar figure cycling at deliberate speed down the Banbury Road on his exceptionally high-seated bicycle, often wearing his academic cap and gown!" He would also regularly cycle to attend Mass at St Aloysius's Church (which after his death was to become the Oxford Oratory) near St Giles on the Woodstock Road, or SS Gregory and Augustine on the same road, in Upper Wolvercote. Tolkien still did some teaching at Leeds in the spring term to help out E. V. Gordon, who had taken on his professorship, and also had some duties to fulfil while his own vacant post of Reader was filled. By April, however, Tolkien had had his final pay packet from Leeds.

In Leeds, Edith had settled into the life of an academic's wife and a mother of young children, pursuing her more domestic interests. In Oxford, her world was separate from much of Tolkien's life – in the then male-dominated world of the university; it would also soon include frequent meetings with C.S. Lewis. Beginning in the thirties, there would be the Inklings. This routine was broken each year by the family vacation. Sometimes the Tolkiens travelled to Lyme Regis, Dorset. Another favourite location was Sidmouth in Devon. A family photo shows Tolkien kneeling in the sand with his children, happily building sand castles.

Whereas at Leeds Edith had enjoyed the company of the wives of Tolkien's colleagues, she found relationships at Oxford very different. One could not imagine happening in the stiff environment of Oxford what had transpired in a Christmas party while at Leeds. The party was organized for all the children of university staff. The plan was for Father Christmas, aka the Vice-Chancellor, to come down a chimney bearing gifts. When he got stuck, all the children could see was a pair of waving legs as he tried to free himself. Suddenly he crashed to the ground amid a dramatic pile of presents.

Edith did not have the advantage of a university education like some dons' wives did. Middle-class norms of the day ruled out her working as a married woman. Besides, she had three young children to mother, with the prospect of more, as expected of a good Catholic wife. Humphrey Carpenter, as Tolkien's official biographer, had access to many private family papers, and observed:

> Edith... was inclined to be shy, for she had led a very
> limited social life in childhood and adolescence... and,
> from her viewpoint as someone who did not know
> Oxford, the University seemed an almost impenetrable
> fortress, a phalanx of imposing buildings where
> important-looking men passed to and fro in gowns, and
> where Ronald disappeared to work each day....[10]

Ronald and Edith's fourth child, Priscilla Mary Reuel Tolkien, was born in 1929. The following year the Tolkien family moved next door to 20 Northmoor Road. This was more spacious than number 22 (after Darnley Road Edith had felt cramped there). Even though she felt more settled with this move, Edith sensed that she was losing something of her husband. Carpenter pointed out:

Family life never entirely regained the equilibrium it had achieved in Leeds. Edith began to feel that she was being ignored by Ronald. In terms of actual hours he was certainly in the house a great deal: much of his teaching was done there, and he was not often out for more than one or two evenings a week. But it was really a matter of his affections. He was very loving and considerate to her, greatly concerned about her health (as she was about his) and solicitous about domestic matters. But she could see that one side of him only came alive when he was in the company of men of his own kind.... [11]

An important source of friction was their Roman Catholic faith. Edith had enjoyed participating in the life of her Anglican church while in Cheltenham years before, and found it hard to convert to the strictures of the new denomination. In particular, she found the practice of confession difficult. For a time she almost stopped attending Mass, and when they returned to Oxford in 1925 she disliked Tolkien taking their children to church. It was difficult for them to discuss the issues in a rational manner, because of Tolkien's emotional attachment to his Church, tied up as it was with his mother's sacrifice in becoming a Roman Catholic. In later years they were able to be reconciled and, although she did not resume regular churchgoing, she was outwardly positive about Catholicism.

Their family remained important to both of them, and they had a number of shared friends. They related to them in their own way – Edith might be talking to one about a child's illness while Tolkien might, at the same time, be commenting, in typical philologist's fashion, about an English place name.

According to Carpenter, regular visitors were well able to adjust to this quirk. Although Edith did not follow Tolkien's fiction as closely as in the wartime years in Staffordshire and Yorkshire, she entered into the family interest when he was writing *The Hobbit* and then *The Lord of the Rings*.

One fine summer's day, probably in 1926, Tolkien and Edith decided upon a family picnic on the banks of the River Cherwell, which joins the Thames in Oxford. At one point Michael, then aged five or so, tripped over the roots of a willow tree and tumbled into the river. Tolkien, wearing his best tennis trousers, immediately jumped in and rescued him. Family holidays were a big event each summer vacation. In both 1927 and 1928, the family holidayed in Lyme Regis, on the Dorset coast. On one of these visits, Tolkien was attracted to a cuckoo clock hanging in their lodgings. He wondered how it worked. As he fiddled with it, the clock broke. The landlady was very annoyed over the incident. As often when relaxed, Tolkien painted and drew assiduously – scenes of the sea, local landscapes, a view of roofs and chimneys, or episodes from places in Middle-earth he was creating or developing. One was of the Elven kingdom of Nargothrond. On the 1928 holiday, they were joined in Lyme Regis by Father Francis Morgan, who kept in touch with the Tolkien family. John, the eldest, was particularly devoted to the Catholic Church, and would eventually become a priest.

In 20 Northmoor Road, relishing the extra space after living next door, Tolkien set up his study. This was important as his students would come to the house for tutorials. Unlike most professors, he didn't have rooms at his college, Pembroke. J.I.M. Stewart used his experience as a student partly to evoke Tolkien's study in his description of his fictional Professor Timbermill's.[12] The study was "the most exciting room", his children John and Priscilla recalled. "The walls were lined with books from floor to ceiling, and it contained a great black lead stove, the source of considerable drama every day: first thing in the morning Ronald would light and draw it, then become distracted by other business, from which he would be aroused by shouts from the neighbours or the postman that the chimney was on fire, black smoke pouring out of it."[13]

On 11 May 1926, Britain was in the grip of a General Strike as a momentous meeting took place. At 4 p.m. there was an "English tea" for the English Department. About six members gathered at Merton College for the event, including C.S. Lewis. He had been appointed a fellow and tutor of Magdalen College, at the same time as Tolkien began his duties as Rawlinson and Bosworth Professor of Anglo-Saxon. He had previously taught philosophy for a year at Oxford as a temporary measure, and was several years younger than Tolkien. It was their first meeting.[14] Also present was the Revd Ronald Fletcher and Margaret Lee, both dons, and George S. Gordon (Merton Professor of English Literature). Tolkien's slight build made Lewis seem taller than he was, and his rather dapper appearance showed up Lewis's wear (the standard tweed coat and flannels) as rather crumpled. Tolkien spoke quickly, Lewis discovered, and you had to listen carefully to catch all his words. He was, in Lewis's impression, "a smooth, pale, fluent little chap".

The meeting might as well have been cocooned from the outside world – there was hardly any talk of the Strike. Tolkien got the conversation around to the English School syllabus.

Lewis was interested to hear his approach; he appeared to wish to bring language and literature studies in the School together more, which was Lewis's own inclination.

Afterwards, Tolkien chatted with Lewis, who quizzed him obliquely. What did Tolkien think of Edmund Spenser (one of Lewis's favourite authors)? Tolkien revealed that he couldn't read the sixteenth-century poet "because of the forms" (that is, presumably, the poetic metres and rhymes he used). What were his views on language and literature in the English School? Tolkien's off-the-cuff comment was that "language is the real thing in the school" (literature was a passionate love of Lewis's; he was one of the best-read of anyone of his generation). Tolkien made matters worse by expressing his high-speed opinion that "all literature is written for the amusement of *men* between thirty and forty". Lewis recorded in his diary that night that according to Tolkien, "We (in the English School) ought to vote ourselves out of existence if we are honest – still the sound-changes and the gobbets [chunks from texts used in examinations] are great fun for the dons." Lewis concluded: "No harm in him: only needs a smack or so." Lewis did however pick up on the fact that "technical hobbies are more in his line". As their friendship developed, the vast range of Tolkien's "technical hobbies" delighted Lewis – his stories and invented languages of Middle-earth, and the chronologies, genealogies, and complex geography that went with them.

The English dons and professors had plenty to talk about. The Oxford English School was then still in its early years as a separate faculty. There were marked differences with its rival and also fledgling Cambridge English School, differences that were to deepen in the next few years. In wishing to bring the teaching of English language and literature together, Tolkien was drawing upon an older view of learning that had its roots in earlier ages. He hoped to install or at least consolidate an attitude in Oxford that would make it natural to be an imaginative writer as well as a don or professor. He attempted in fact to rehabilitate what he yearned after as a lost consciousness, an older unity of thinking, imagination, and belief. This was a wholeness that he found in the mystery of language itself. Myth and story was embodied in language.

By the end of 1929, a little over three years after their first meeting, Tolkien's proposed changes to the Oxford English School had Lewis's support, changes that would integrate language and literature to a greater extent. Controversially, the changes would stop the syllabus with the Romantics at around 1830. After this point, Tolkien argued, the modern reader was familiar with the predominant world view of literary authors and, thus, did not need the kind of help teachers in the English School were best suited to give. This was help in obscure texts, shifts in the meaning of words, and in tasting the imaginative worlds of previous ages, especially the imaginative splendour of the Middle Ages. Many years later, C.S. Lewis looked back on this period. "During the years 1925–35 [Tolkien] was, more than any other single man, responsible for closing the old rift between 'literature' and 'philology' in English Studies at Oxford and thus giving the existing school its characteristic temper. His unique insight at once into the language of poetry and the poetry of language qualified him for this task."[15]

Philosopher John Mabbott, a don at that time, pointed out the astonishing intellectual isolation, in some respects, of Oxford then. In his *Oxford Memories* he wrote:

Oxford philosophy, as we found it, was completely
inbred. It had practically no contacts with Cambridge,
or the Continent, or America. The traditional doctrine
was Hegelian idealism... The basic issue was between
the idealists and their view that reality is spiritual
and therefore that the world around us is akin to
or determined by mind, and our realists... holding
that the objects of knowledge and perception are
independent of mind.[16]

Idealism was linked for many with Christianity, or with
spiritual views that opposed a rapidly spreading naturalism (or
materialism). The idealists typically held that physical objects
can have no existence unless in a mind that is conscious of
them. For them the divine mind and the human mind had
fundamental similarities. When Tolkien and Lewis first met,
the two men had radically opposing world views, though
Lewis was moving away from a materialist view to a form of
idealism. Tolkien was a traditional supernaturalist, who had
of course believed the orthodox doctrines of Christianity
since childhood.

Through C.S. Lewis, Tolkien was discovering a friendship
that would have important similarities with the one he
had previously enjoyed with Christopher Wiseman of the
T.C.B.S. Since the war, the two had seen little of each other
and the friendship weakened as they developed their careers.
In fact, Wiseman in 1926 became headmaster of Queen's
College, Taunton, a Methodist public school. Though not
yet a supernaturalist and Christian like Wiseman was,
Lewis was from a north of Ireland Protestant tradition that
contrasted with Tolkien's Roman Catholicism. Lewis had

Right: J.R.R. Tolkien considered his rural childhood and Sarehole Mill as "The Shire".

Below: J.R.R. Tolkien lived with his mother and brother in the cottage to the right in Sarehole, then known as The Cottages, Gracewell.

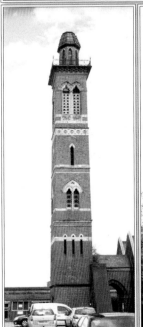

Above: After their mother's death, the orphaned brothers lived with their aunt, Beatrice Suffield, in this house in Stirling Road, Edgbaston.

Far Left: The Waterworks Tower is visible above the houses in Stirling Road, and is one of Edgbaston's twin towers, believed locally to have inspired Tolkien's Two Towers.

Left: The so-called "Perrott's Folly" dominates Edgbaston's skyline. It is an elegant eighteenth century relic associated with lost parkland.

Left: Founded by Cardinal Newman, the Birmingham Oratory became the spiritual home of Mabel Tolkien and her sons.

Below: The Ivy Bush, Edgbaston. A pub of this name was familiar to the inhabitants of Hobbiton, in The Shire. Ronald and Hilary Tolkien passed it frequently.

Below: Woodland Cottage, Rednal, was beside the Lickey Hills in Worcestershire. Mabel spent the last part of her short life here. The area was a favourite place for the brothers.

Above: Lyme Regis, Dorset. The building prominent to the left was the location of The Three Cups Hotel, at which Ronald and Hilary Tolkien stayed with their guardian, Father Francis Morgan.

Left: The Cobb, Lyme Regis. On holidays to the Dorset coast as a boy, Ronald explored the shore and developed a love for the sea.

Above: During a holiday in Whitby, on the Yorkshire coast, 18-year old Ronald sketched the leftmost (west) end of the ruins of the historic Whitby Abbey, associated with St Hilda, the poet Caedmon, the Synod of Whitby, and much else.

Right: J.R.R. Tolkien attended Exeter College, Turl Street, while an undergraduate at Oxford.

Above: Exeter College quadrangle with the Chapel to the right.

Above: Edith Bratt shared 15 Victoria Street, Warwick, with her cousin Jennie Grove while engaged to Tolkien. The young couple developed a deep affection for the town.

Left: As an undergraduate, J.R.R. Tolkien had some of his lectures at The Taylorian Institute.

Above: J.R.R. Tolkien and Edith Bratt married in the Church of St Mary Immaculate in Warwick.

Above: Typical military accommodation during the First World War. Huge training camps were built on Cannock Chase, Staffordshire, and Tolkien was based here after his marriage.

Left: Essex Bridge crossing the River Trent at Great Haywood, Staffordshire. It is the longest extant packhorse bridge in England. Edith Tolkien, together with her cousin, rented accommodation here to be near Tolkien's military camp.

Above: While Tolkien was posted by the army to Holderness, Yorkshire, he had temporary living quarters near Roos where Edith joined him. They explored the surrounding countryside.

Above: J.R.R. Tolkien and his close friends in the T.C.B.S. met for a "Council of Lichfield" at the George Hotel. It proved to be the last time they would all meet. Soon after two of them were killed in action in France.

Below: Tolkien was posted once more to a military camp in Cannock Chase. Edith, their first child John, and her cousin found delightful accommodation nearby at an isolated cottage called 'Gipsy Green', on the private Teddersley Estate.

Above: It was probably in Dents Garth Wood, Roos, that Edith danced in a clearing and helped to inspire one of J.R.R. Tolkien's greatest stories, that of Beren and Lúthien.

Left: Upon returning to Oxford after the war, Tolkien worked for the Oxford English Dictionary, then based in the Old Ashmolean building, on Broad Street.

Bottom left: Tolkien lived at 50 St John Street, while working for the Oxford English Dictionary.

Below: Tolkien moved to larger accommodation in Pusey Street (then named Alfred Street). The street opens into St Giles.

Above: The Great Hall, University of Leeds. Beginning in 1920, Tolkien taught at Leeds, first as Reader and then as Professor of English Language.

Top right: Tolkien's home, 2 Darnley Road, north Leeds, from the side.

Above: While Tolkien was teaching in Leeds, the family took holidays in Filey, on the Yorkshire coast, which inspired poems and the story, *Roverandom*.

Left: While on holiday in Filey, the family walked to Flamborough Head to view a wrecked German submarine.

Right: What was "Bag End" farm, near Inkberrow, Worcestershire, visited by Tolkien during his five years in Leeds.

Above: The dead end lane to what was "Bag End" farm still exists today.

Above: On Addison's Walk, Tolkien and H.V.D. Dyson had a long night conversation with C.S. Lewis that helped persuade him of the truth of Christian belief.

Left: Broad Street, Oxford, with Blackwell's Bookshop and The White Horse pub on the right.

Right: The front of New Building, Magdalen College, where C.S. Lewis had his rooms and tutored, and where Tolkien and others of the Inklings often met on Thursday evenings.

Above: The Eagle and Child pub in Oxford's St Giles. Tolkien would often meet with his friends, the Inklings, on Tuesday mornings in the snug "The Rabbit Room," at the rear of the pub (top right).

Above: An older pub sign which used to hang outside The Eagle and the Child.

Left: St Aloysius' Roman Catholic Church, in Woodstock Road (now part of The Oxford Oratory), was one of Tolkien's places of worship.

Left: During retirement Tolkien and his wife Edith often stayed in Hotel Miramar, Bournemouth, eventually moving to the seaside resort.

Right: On their grave stone, Tolkien and his wife Edith are called Beren and Lúthien.

been brought up in a Protestant area on the fringe of Belfast called Strandtown, with his father a strong Unionist. Though Lewis's upbringing took place before Partition and the secession of the south in 1922, political feelings were strong and the rhetoric fiery. Lewis and Wiseman were also alike in being committed to a scientific realism. Thus, for each, the grounds for truth were based on verifiable evidence. Though Tolkien held to the truth of Christianity in their sense, he also held to the authority of the Roman Catholic Church, and its extra-biblical decrees such as the Assumption of Mary (to give a twentieth-century example, with the Papal decree of the infallibility of the doctrine on All Saints' Day, 1950). With both Lewis and Wiseman, Tolkien had a deep and abiding friendship that was fundamental, and which nevertheless had its ups and downs, as is common in such relationships. In one case, Wiseman eventually felt neglected by Tolkien; in the other, Tolkien by Lewis.

It was not only in philosophy that Oxford in the twenties had an ethos from the nineteenth century. It was also, in the study of language and literature, still gripped by the model of philology – the historical and comparative study of language and its embodiment in literature. The philologist at his best was summed up in Tolkien. He had unusually broad concerns, such as the serious writing of fantasy and fairy story, as well as a passionate love of language. One day Tolkien and Lewis would even plan to collaborate on a book on language, a project that never materialized.

For Tolkien, writing and speaking are tied up together in the mystery of human language. In his essay "The Oxford English School", Tolkien made clear that he regarded both literary and linguistic approaches as too narrow to gain a full response to works of art.[17] He felt that this was particularly true of early literary works, which are very distant from contemporary understanding. Philology was a necessary dimension of both literary and linguistic approaches. It alone could give each a proper depth of response. As time had gone on, it had become clear (especially to friends like Coghill and C.S. Lewis, who became Inklings) that Tolkien's long study and teaching of languages was intimately related to his imaginative creations. In a letter to W.H. Auden, written many years later, he confessed that he always had had a "sensibility to linguistic pattern which affects me emotionally like colour or music".

One of the many issues that Tolkien discussed with friends was that of the nature of language: its changes over time, how it revealed an ancient consciousness in human beings that was not fragmented as in modern times, and the way language carried and was shaped by mythology. Owen Barfield was a contemporary of Tolkien who was a very close friend of C.S. Lewis. Though, like Lewis, he was over six years younger than Tolkien, he had already developed outstanding insights into the character of language, and would continue to do so through his long life. Tolkien read Owen Barfield's *Poetic Diction* (1928); Lewis may have lent him a copy. What particularly struck Tolkien was Barfield's view that in ancient times thinking was not detached from participation in the world. In Barfield's carefully argued view, the way people experienced reality as a seamless whole was embodied at that time in their language. In a way, their thought was completely poetic in the sense of being non-abstract and figurative. (An idea of what Barfield meant can be found in William Golding's 1955 novel, *The Inheritors,* which is told from the perspective of Neanderthal man.) In an undated letter to Barfield, possibly written in 1929, Lewis observed:

> You might like to know that when Tolkien dined with me the other night he said à-propos of something quite different that your conception of the ancient semantic unity had modified his whole outlook and that he was almost just going to say something in a lecture when your conception stopped him in time. "It is one of those things", he said, "that when you've once seen it there are all sorts of things you can never say again.[18]

Barfield's complex book was one of the most important single influences on both Tolkien and Lewis, though for each to some extent it may have clarified and focused ideas and insights they already had. For instance, Tolkien had already concluded that mythology could not be separated from language, and vice versa. One of the main observations that Barfield made in *Poetic Diction*, and other books, is how the very way we see the world has changed over time. It is a kind of "chronological snobbery" (to use a phrase of Lewis's) to consider the modern view superior to all past perceptions of reality.

Tolkien and Lewis also shared a fervent interest in Old and Middle English literature. Though the range of Lewis's literary interests was far wider than Tolkien's, Lewis was nevertheless well read in this specific period. Undoubtedly poems such as *Pearl, Sir Orfeo,* and *Beowulf* frequently came up in their conversations. Tolkien is likely to have shown or read Lewis his unfinished verse translation of *Beowulf,* made while he was in Leeds. He certainly showed his friend the first of two prose translations of *Beowulf* he made in the late twenties or early thirties, as the typescript contains amendments in what is more than probably Lewis's handwriting. This indicates that Lewis read and commented on the translation. Tolkien incorporated the emendations into his final version.

Yet Tolkien was still at this time working to integrate his thought and his imagination. The main audience for his stories was his children, and over the years he had told a variety of them. In the twenties there was no general adult readership for fantasy. There was some truth in his throwaway comment to Lewis that literature was meant for men between thirty and forty. Tolkien sought to rehabilitate fairy stories as reading for adults rather than being relegated to the safety of the nursery. Tales he loved, such as *Beowulf*, had once upon a time been standard fare for adults; indeed, they did not embarrass tough warriors. According to Austin Olney, Tolkien's American editor at Houghton Mifflin for many years,

> During the 1920s and 1930s Tolkien's imagination
> was running along two distinct courses that did not
> meet. On one side were the stories composed for the
> amusement of his children. On the other were the
> grander themes, sometimes Arthurian or Celtic, but
> usually associated with his own legends…. Something
> was lacking, something that would bring the two sides
> of the imagination together and produce a story that was
> at once heroic and mythical and at the same time tuned
> to the popular imagination.[19]

The idea that he was going to create, almost single-handedly, a global adult readership for fairy story and fantasy, and for myth on a heroic scale, would have been beyond even Tolkien's imagination. Yet he had a vision, born in his association with his T.C.B.S. friends, which carried him gradually forward. He was soon to recognize a remarkably similar vision in C.S. Lewis and, to varying extents, some friends they had in common.

In the summer of 1925, just before he started the new Chair at Oxford, Tolkien began writing a poetic version of his story about Beren and Lúthien. This became one of the chief stories of "The Silmarillion", briefly retold in song by Aragorn in *The Lord of the Rings*. Like *The Lord of the Rings* it is a heroic romance, though on a smaller scale. Tolkien worked on both poetic and prose versions, though none of the poetic versions was ever completed. In A.N. Wilson's view, "Though at times the verse is technically imperfect, it is full of passages of quite stunning beauty; and the overall conception must make it, though unfinished, one of the most remarkable poems written in English in the twentieth century."[20]

The tale of Beren and Lúthien is set in Beleriand, during the First Age of Middle-earth. Lúthien was the daughter of the Elven King Thingol, ruler of Doriath, and Queen Melian, and thus immortal. Beren was "a mortal man doomed to die". Many of Tolkien's characteristic themes emerge in this story. Through the eventual marriage of Beren and Lúthien, an Elven quality was preserved through their children into future generations – right into the Fourth Age, when humankind became ascendant, and the Elves declined. This theme is repeated in *The Lord of the Rings* with the union of Arwen and Aragorn. Throughout the Ages of Middle-earth the story of Beren and Lúthien brought hope and consolation both to Elves and to those humans who were faithful against the powers of darkness. This hope is often expressed in *The Lord of the Rings,* by Aragorn and many others.

Tolkien saw the tale of Beren and Lúthien as the central story of "The Silmarillion", the key to its interlocking themes and events. The story had the potential to be told in a detail and length approaching that of *The Lord of the Rings.* As it was, Tolkien never fully finished it. Late in 1929, he gave a large portion of the poem to his friend C.S. Lewis to read, who commented on it in depth. While in the process of reading it, Lewis wrote to Tolkien:

> I can quite honestly say that it is ages since I have had an evening of such delight: and the personal interest of reading a friend's work had very little to do with it. I should have enjoyed it just as well as if I'd picked it up in a bookshop, by an unknown author. The two things that come out clearly are the sense of reality in the background and the mythical value: the essence of a myth being that it should have no taint of allegory to the maker and yet should suggest incipient allegories to the reader.[21]

What Lewis says of that early poetry from "The Silmarillion" is also strikingly true of Tolkien's later work, *The Lord of the Rings*, with its presence of myth, and its background of definite places and history. Tolkien somehow creates a sense of reality in his imagined world.

Early the following year, Lewis offered comments on the unfinished poem in the form of a mock academic commentary, which ran to fourteen pages. He presented the commentary in the form of several spoof literary critics, representing various critical positions including analysis of sources – Schick, Schuffer, Pumpernickel, Bentley, and Peabody. He had already discovered that Tolkien's response to criticism of his work was either to ignore it, or to go back to the beginning and start a total rewriting. He felt that the work had considerable merit, but would benefit from some changes – certainly not a radical rewrite.

Sharing his mythology with Lewis was an important step for Tolkien in finding an adult readership (then nearly non-existent) for fairy tales. Fairies for Tolkien were the noble Elves of Middle-earth, such as the beautiful Lúthien, and her parents, King Thingol and Queen Melian. He took another tentative step by presenting a paper called "A Secret Vice" to an Oxford society in 1931. This paper is a particular interest because of a number of references to his life. Tolkien speaks of the pleasure of inventing languages, and believes that this technical linguistic "hobby" is natural in childhood. It can survive to adulthood: he gives examples of his own invention, including Elvish languages.

Tolkien had already intrigued Lewis by alluding to his linguistic and writing "hobbies". When Tolkien invited him to come along to the Coalbiters, he gladly accepted. This was an informal reading club Tolkien had initiated at Oxford in the spring of 1926. Its purpose was to explore Icelandic literature such as the *Poetic Edda*. The name referred to those who crowd so close to the fire in winter that they seem to "bite the coal". Nevill Coghill, now a research fellow in English at Exeter College, also soon joined the group. They sometimes met in pubs, an Oxford habit of donnish friends, but often in the High Street house of John Bryson, an English tutor and lecturer at Merton College. Lewis noted to a friend that they were reading *Sir Gawain and the Green Knight* in the original Middle English and learning Old Icelandic. He also reported that the Coalbiters had already read legends such as the *Poetic Edda* and the *Volsunga Saga*. Next term they were going to read the *Laxdala Saga*.

Tolkien was the most fluent of the members; he could faultlessly translate the Icelandic sagas they studied straight from the page. Lewis, Coghill, and most of the others made much slower progress, maybe managing just half a page at a time. Tolkien was in his element with such stories that evoked a vast, northern world, with wide, pale skies, dragons, courage against the darkness, and vulnerable gods. There were in the group some seeds of the future Inklings, the literary group that was, to an extent, to become for Tolkien a replacement for the grievous loss of the T.C.B.S. Some members were future Inklings – Lewis, Nevill Coghill, and Tolkien himself. In major ways, however, it did not resemble the Inklings at all, particularly in being completely made up of dons, professors, and similar, and meeting two or three times a term for a very specific purpose: to become more familiar with Old Icelandic, a close relation of Old English.

As a result of the Coalbiter gatherings, Tolkien and Lewis were soon meeting and sometimes talking far into the night. At some stage, Tolkien started to call Lewis by his self-chosen name of Jack, used only by close friends and family. It eventually became a regular habit for Tolkien to drop by Magdalen College around mid-morning on Mondays (a day when Lewis had no students). The two friends usually crossed the High Street and went to the Eastgate Hotel or to a nearby public house for a drink. Sometimes they met at Tolkien's home in Northmoor Road. (Edith was used to her husband's late returns and his writing into the early hours of the morning – they had separate bedrooms in order not to disturb her sleep.) In a letter to a close Belfast friend, Arthur Greeves, in December 1929, Lewis recorded that after one meeting Tolkien came back with him to his college rooms and "sat discoursing of the gods and giants of Asgard for three hours". Sometimes they talked university English School politics. Other times they commented on each other's poems. They might drift into theology or "the state of the nation". On rare occasions they simply played with bawdy and pun. Among other things, they plotted in establishing a coherent undergraduate syllabus for the English School at Oxford, as mentioned earlier. After Lewis's death Dame Helen Gardner wrote:

> Perhaps one of the most significant of [Lewis's]
> contributions to the study of English literature at
> Oxford was the part he played with his friend Professor
> J.R.R. Tolkien in establishing a syllabus for the Final
> Honour School which embodied his belief in the value
> of medieval (especially Old English) literature, his
> conviction that a proper study of modern literature
> required the linguistic training that the study of earlier
> literature gave, and his sense of the continuity of English
> literature and the syllabus, which remained in force for
> over twenty years, was in many ways an admirable one.[22]

Tolkien's reformed syllabus was accepted, in fact, by 1931, bringing together "Lang." and "Lit.".

These frequent conversations were to prove of utmost importance both for the two men's writings, and for Lewis's eventual conversion to the Christian faith. The Ulsterman

Lewis remarked in *Surprised by Joy*: "Friendship with [J.R.R. Tolkien] marked the breakdown of two old prejudices. At my first coming into the world I had been (implicitly) warned never to trust a Papist, and at my first coming into the English Faculty (explicitly) never to trust a philologist. Tolkien was both."[23] (Lewis often referred to Catholics as "Papists", a mark of his Ulster heritage, a label Tolkien did not find easy.) It is clear that, from the beginning, Lewis recognized Tolkien's remarkable literary gifts. On Tolkien's side, too, there was much gratefulness.

At this time it was their usual practice (common then) to call each other by surname. Tolkien's first names other than "Ronald" were not known to Lewis as late as 1957. Tolkien's conversational style was captured by his friend: "He is the most unmanageable man (in conversation) I've ever met. He will talk to you alright, but the subject of his remarks will be whatever happens to be interesting him at the moment, which might be anything from M.[iddle] E.[nglish] words to Oxford [English School] politics." Tolkien too, long after, recalled conversation with Lewis at this period: "C.S. Lewis was one of the only three persons who have so far read all or a considerable part of my 'mythology' of the First and Second Ages..." He also remembered reading aloud to Lewis "The Silmarillion" so far as he had then written it. Tolkien was not now so alone in the world.

10

Of Hobbits and Inklings

J.R.R. Tolkien's story began with a word that seemed to pop up out of nowhere. The word was "Hobbit". One summer's day – probably sometime in the late 1920s – Tolkien had beside him two piles of papers. One was made up of unmarked School Certificate examination papers, and the other of those he had laboured to mark. It was not a task he relished. He found it necessary to supplement the income he received from his professorial duties in order to pay the stream of household bills, including medical ones from various family ailments. We can easily imagine him at his desk, a pen in hand, a Toby jug sprouting pipes and a wooden tobacco jar nearby – for he told the story many times of the birth of his classic tale, *The Hobbit*. Tolkien was, likely enough, silent as he fulfilled his task, except for an occasional muttered, "O lor'." The story goes that he came across a blank page on one of the scripts. (At this point, his face would light up in the telling.) Suddenly, he scribbled across it: "In a hole in the ground there lived a hobbit."

At this stage he had no idea about what a "Hobbit" was. As always, names generated a story in his mind. Eventually he decided that he had better find out what these mysterious Hobbits were like. He felt that he had stumbled across an as yet unknown word in the English language. Had he coined it, or had he discovered the word "Hobbit"?

Though Tolkien probably began writing down the story in 1930, his eldest sons, John and Michael, remembered the story being told to them before that. This would therefore have been one or two years before when they were aged about eleven and nine respectively. It is likely that various oral forms of the story merged into the more finished written draft. It was common for Tolkien to tell his children stories. What is significant from these indistinct memories is that *The Hobbit* began as a tale told by a father to his young children. It was consciously written as a children's story and this fact shapes its style. Roger Lancelyn Green, who knew Tolkien, wrote in his book *Tellers of Tales* that *The Hobbit* "grew out of the stories told to his own children". One source of inspiration, revealed years later by Tolkien, was E.A. Wyke-Smith's engaging children's fantasy, *The Marvellous Land of Snergs* (1927), in which Snergs have some similarities with Hobbits, including their size: "only slightly taller than the average table but broad in the shoulders and of great strength".

At first the story was independent of Tolkien's burgeoning mythological cycle, "The Silmarillion", and was only later incorporated into his invented world and history in the process of writing. The tale, in fact, introduced Hobbits into Middle-earth, dramatically affecting the course of events there. *The Hobbit* belongs to the Third Age of Middle-earth, and chronologically precedes *The Lord of the Rings*. In later years, Tolkien did attempt adult versions of the story.

One was a short piece that he mostly left out of *The Lord of the Rings,* called "The Quest of Erebor".[1] The other was a couple of chapters and various insertions of what started as a rewrite of *The Hobbit* in 1960 that was soon abandoned.[2] Peter Jackson's film retelling of *The Hobbit* in effect continues such a recasting for an adult audience.

By the beginning of 1933 Tolkien was able to hand Lewis a sheaf of papers to read. It was a largely typed-up draft of what became *The Hobbit: or There and Back Again.* Scholars are divided over whether the story was then reasonably complete, but not whether it was an early draft. Christopher Tolkien points out that chapters at the end of the initial writing "were rather roughly done, and not typed out at all".[3]) Lewis described his reaction to it in another of his frequent letters to Arthur Greeves: "Reading his fairy tale has been uncanny – it is so exactly like what we would both have longed to write (or read) in 1916: so that one feels he is not making it up but merely describing the same world into which all three of us have the entry." Lewis had already written to Greeves in rosiest terms of his friendship with Tolkien, comparing it favourably with their own – like them, Lewis said, Tolkien had grown up on William Morris and George MacDonald. In a letter a few weeks later he mentions Tolkien sharing their love of "romance" literature, and in the same sense: "He agreed that for what we meant by romance there must be at least the hint of another world – one must hear the horns of elfland."

Tolkien also lent a copy to a couple of others. One was Elaine Griffiths, a former B.Litt. student he had been supervising. As it happened, she was enlisted to help in the revision of a modern translation of *Beowulf.* Tolkien was overseeing her work on the translation, and had agreed to write a brief introduction. Her publisher, George Allen and Unwin, sent one of their staff, Susan Dagnell, to see Elaine Griffiths in Oxford in connection with this project. During her visit, she heard about Tolkien's story – perhaps she saw the typescript in her client's lodgings. As a result, she seems to have been lent it by Elaine Griffiths (most likely seeing Tolkien later that day and asking his permission to take it with her). Her reading of *The Hobbit* convinced her that it should be published, and she wrote to Tolkien asking him if he would finish it, so that it could be considered for publication. When he eventually sent in a final typescript, Stanley Unwin, head of publishing, and two outside readers, including his ten-year-old son, Raynor, read it. Raynor sagely concluded his report with the comment that the book "is good and should appeal to all children between the ages of 5 and 9".[4] The boy earned a fee of one shilling for reading the typescript.

The Hobbit was eventually published on 21 September 1937, complete with Tolkien's own illustrations; the initial printing was 1,500 copies. Tolkien sent out copies to some friends and relations, including his aunt Jane Neave, his brother Hilary, Jennie Grove, Elaine Griffiths, and Mrs Ruth Smith, the mother of his dear friend Geoffrey Bache Smith, who had died in battle over twenty years before. A sister of another T.C.B.S. member, Christopher Wiseman, begged Tolkien for a copy, on the grounds that she had taken a vow of poverty with her Roman Catholic religious order, the Benedictines of the Immaculate Conception. Mary St John, OSB, who belonged to Oulton Abbey, offered to pay for the book with prayers for Tolkien and his family! W.H. Auden, when he reviewed *The Fellowship of the Ring* some years later for *The New York Times,* wrote: "In my opinion, [*The Hobbit*] is one of the best children's stories of this century."[5]

The publishers soon realized a reprint would be necessary and that readers would demand more about the Hobbits. It was reprinted just before Christmas that year. Stanley Unwin pressed Tolkien for another book. In November of that year, Tolkien had sent Unwin the four chapters he had written of a new story, "The Lost Road" (which he never was to complete). At the same time he offered his publisher much of "The Silmarillion" material, which he described as his "private and beloved nonsense". He agreed with Unwin that a "sequel or successor to The Hobbit is called for", but was at a loss about what more Hobbits could do. He confessed this in a letter of 16 December, but only three days later, on 19 December, he told Unwin of a breakthrough: "I have written the first chapter of a new story about Hobbits." This turned out to be the opening of *The Lord of the Rings,* published seventeen years later. Readers had a long wait ahead of them.

At the time of publication, Lewis reviewed his friend's book for *The Times Literary Supplement*: "Prediction is dangerous," he warned, "but *The Hobbit* may well prove a classic." Another critic, in the *New Statesman*, remarked of Tolkien: "It is a triumph that the genus Hobbit, which he himself has invented, rings just as real as the time-hallowed genera of Goblin, Troll, and Elf." Instead of a creation of character as we find it in standard modern fiction, much of the personality of Bilbo derives from his character as a Hobbit, just as we identify Gandalf in character as a Wizard, or Thorin Oakenshield as a Dwarf. Tolkien sustains the collective qualities of these different mythological species with great skill.

The title of *The Hobbit* refers to its unlikely hero, Mr Bilbo Baggins. Though bourgeois, he was a creature of paradox, summed up in his unchosen role as a burglar in the story. Hobbits aimed at having a good reputation with their peers – not only by being comfortably off, but by not having any adventures or doing anything unexpected. Bilbo's house was the typical dwelling place of a wealthy Hobbit. It was not a worm-filled, dirty, damp hole, but a comfortable, many-roomed underground home. Its long hall, which connected all the rooms, had "panelled walls, and floors tiled and carpeted, provided with polished chairs, and lots and lots of pegs for hats and coats – the hobbit was fond of visitors".

Bilbo's reputation was ruined when he was suddenly caught up in a quest for dragon's treasure. He reluctantly found this more congenial than he ever thought. A whole new world was opened up to him, and in later years he even became somewhat of a scholar, translating and retelling tales from the older days. The quest also developed his character, though he always retained the quality of homeliness associated with Hobbits and the Shire, where they lived.

In *The Hobbit,* a party of Dwarves, thirteen in number, were on a quest for their long-lost treasure, which was jealously guarded by a dragon, Smaug. Their leader was the great Thorin Oakenshield. They employed Bilbo Baggins as their master burglar to steal the treasure, at the recommendation of the Wizard Gandalf the Grey.

As their journey unfolded, the Dwarves became increasingly thankful for the fact that they had employed him, despite initial misgivings, as he got them out of many scrapes. He seemed to have extraordinary luck. At one point in the adventure, Bilbo was knocked unconscious in a tunnel under the Misty Mountains, and left behind in the darkness by the rest of the party.

When he came to, Bilbo discovered an ancient ring lying beside him in the tunnel. It was a ring of ultimate power, but at this stage Bilbo was to discover only its magical property of invisibility. After a battle of riddles with Gollum, a slimy, small, underground creature with large, pale eyes who had lost the ring, Bilbo escaped, seemingly by luck, by slipping it on. Following the vengeful Gollum, who could not see him, he found his way out of the mountains, on the other side.

After the encounter with Gollum, the plucky Bilbo eventually led the party successfully to the dragon's treasure, and the scaly monster perished while attacking nearby Lake-town.

At the end, Bilbo and Gandalf journeyed back to the peaceful Shire – the Hobbit had gone "there and back again". Bilbo decided to refuse most of his share of the treasure, having seen the results of greed. The events had in fact changed him forever, but even more, the ring he secretly possessed would shape the events in due course to be recorded in *The Lord of the Rings*.

Bilbo's discovery of the ring was eventually to provide Tolkien with the link between *The Hobbit* and its grand sequel, *The Lord of the Rings*. However, Tolkien realized he had to partially rewrite chapter 5 of the former book to provide proper continuity between the two works over the great significance of the ruling ring. He drafted the revision ten years after the publication of *The Hobbit*, in the midst of finalizing *The Lord of the Rings*. The new edition, incorporating the revised chapter, first appeared in 1951.

In 1932, while writing *The Hobbit*, Tolkien bought his first car, a Morris Cowley known as "Old Jo", after its number plate, JO 9184. (He later abandoned car ownership on principle, because of the environmental impact he could see on the English countryside of massive car ownership and production.) Owning the car led to an eventful family trip to visit Hilary Tolkien in Evesham, in which two of the tyres deflated and Tolkien's erratic driving partially demolished a drystone wall near Chipping Norton. The consequences of having a car inspired another children's story, *Mr Bliss* (illustrated in colour throughout by Tolkien himself), and not in fact published until 1982 because of publishing costs at the time. The car itself in the story may owe something also to a toy car belonging to Tolkien's youngest son, Christopher. It is the tale of Mr Bliss, a man noted for his tall hats, who lives in a tall house, and about his adventures after buying a bright yellow car for five shillings. A minor character called "Gaffer Gamgee" appears briefly. In *The Lord of the Rings* this becomes the name of Sam's father. The name was first used by Tolkien for an old man the family came across on holiday in Lamorna Cove in Cornwall, during the late summer of 1932. He was well known locally there for exchanging gossip and for his weather lore. Tolkien dubbed him Gaffer Gamgee ("Gamgee" of course being the local name from Tolkien's childhood for cotton wool). In *Mr Bliss,* the bright yellow car at one point crashes into a garden wall at the bottom of a hill, upending its occupants into a garden where a family are about to eat a picnic. For Tolkien's original readers, his children, this was likely to have been recognized as an allusion to the drystone wall near Chipping Norton!

The strange figure of Tom Bombadil, "master of wood, water and hill", also saw life during this period. He was a nature spirit, mastered by none and refusing possession himself. Like the biblical Adam, he was a name-giver.

Tom Bombadil started out as a Dutch doll belonging to Michael Tolkien as a young child, with a splendid feather in its hat. He became the hero of "The Adventures of Tom Bombadil", which Tolkien published in a poetry collection in 1934. Tom Bombadil eventually re-emerged as a significant figure in *The Lord of the Rings*. He gave to the ponies of the Hobbits names that they "answered to for the rest of their lives". Like the Wizards, his appearance was that of a man, though, unlike them, he had been in Middle-earth from earliest days. Tolkien's talent for songs, ballads, and witty riddles, voiced in Tom Bombadil, fitted well into a Hobbitish setting. In a letter to his publisher in 1937 Tolkien spoke of Tom Bombadil as the spirit of the vanishing countryside of Berkshire and Oxfordshire. He was a very timely figure, refusing to dominate nature, who could well serve as the patron saint of the good scientist.

Now that they had a car, these two counties endued with Tom Bombadil's spirit had become accessible for family day trips from Oxford. At weekends, they were able to head to Berkshire and explore the Ridgeway walk above the Vale of the White Horse, to see the White Horse of Uffington etched millennia ago onto the green chalk Downs, Dragon Hill below it, and nearby Wayland's Smithy, a huge Neolithic long barrow with burial chambers. (Following boundary changes in 1974 this area is now in Oxfordshire.) To the northwest of Oxfordshire, there were the extraordinary Rollright Stones, near Moreton-in-Marsh. Everywhere in the two shires there were picturesque villages full of history. Edith had been rather alarmed by the adventures encountered travelling that first time to Evesham in the big, second-hand car, in which the wall had been damaged. Their later short excursions by car however changed all that. Edith began to enjoy the car-riding. The family had other days or afternoons out on a punt hired for the season. Setting off on the River Cherwell, they might drift down to Magdalen Bridge, beside C.S. Lewis's college, or pole their way upriver in the direction of Islip, where they might picnic somewhere on the riverbank.

In 1938, Tolkien read a new story, *Farmer Giles of Ham*, to an undergraduate society at Worcester College, instead of the announced academic paper on fairy stories, which was not yet ready. Though suitable for children, it had felt its way towards being an adult story, which is why perhaps Tolkien saw it as an adequate substitute for the academic paper. Not published until 1950, this light-hearted short story is subtitled "The Rise and Wonderful Adventures of Farmer Giles, Lord of Tame, Count of Worminghall and King of the Little Kingdom". It begins with a mock-scholarly foreword about its supposed authorship, translation from Latin, and the extent of the "Little Kingdom" in "a dark period of the history of Britain", before the days of King Arthur, in the valley of the Thames.

This humorous story, though on the surface very different from the tales of Middle-earth, is characteristic of Tolkien in its themes. The story's inspiration is linguistic: it provides a spoof explanation for the name of an actual village to the east of Oxford, a favourite of Tolkien's that the family had visited on one of their excursions, called Worminghall. The Little Kingdom has similarities with the Shire, particularly in Farmer Giles's sheltered and homely life. He is like a complacent Hobbit, with unexpected qualities.

Family outings, and summer seaside holidays, were important, it seems, to Tolkien's stability. His professorship at Oxford was a demanding round of lectures, tutorials, supervision of postgraduate B.Litt. students, and committee and other administrative meetings. He tended to write his fiction and poetry, and to paint and draw, in fervent bursts during holidays. Weekend excursions with his family allowed him to give them his full attention. He sometimes entertained at children's parties at a nearby Oxford convent in the summer and at Christmas. There were some signs that his emotional life was fragile, and could crack open. He had sometimes joked that his German name "Tolkien" could mean *tollkühn*, "foolhardy", alluding to that recklessly brave ancestor who was said to have taken part in an unofficial raid during the Siege of Vienna in 1529, capturing the Turkish Sultan's standard.

On one occasion, in late summer 1938, he came close to having a nervous breakdown. Humphrey Carpenter reveals, in his official biography, that Tolkien would reserve his diaries for setting down some of his darkest and most troubled thoughts. His fiction, with admirable power, explores some of the deepest human struggles, such as the inevitability of death. In a lecture he was preparing, he would speak of the "escapism" of fantasy being the breakout of the prisoner rather than the flight of the deserter. The escapes of fantasy pertain to "grim and terrible" matters such as "hunger, thirst, poverty, pain, sorrow, injustice, death".[6] John Lawlor, a former student of Tolkien's, paints a brief but inspiring portrait of his teacher's qualities and kindness in his *Memories and Reflections,* yet also points to the emotional turmoil Tolkien sometimes suffered. Describing him as having "his being in two worlds", he remembers Tolkien's seemingly bottomless grief on seeing his undergraduate son Christopher's final results. There was also an occasion later, after the war, that was far more dramatic. Alluding to Tolkien's play on his name as "foolhardy", Lawlor reveals how "his habitually mild and benevolently quizzical temper was capable of absolutely volcanic upheaval". Tolkien's colleague and fellow Inkling C.L. Wrenn, whose wife Agnes was a good friend of Edith's, had laboured long and hard, despite illness, to create the International Association of University Professors of English (IAUPE). The Association began at a conference held at Magdalen College in 1950:

> Wrenn's custom throughout the evenings of the Conference was to invite to the High Table in Magdalen those members who had been particularly helpful in arranging and conducting matters, leading them back after dinner for coffee and something stronger in the Conference office – the ground floor of St Swithun's. Comfortably seated and contentedly gathered around Wrenn, the participants heard the door thrown open and a wild-eyed Tolkien – veritably "tollkühn", the foolhardy one – burst in, to harangue Wrenn for his unseemly action in so using Magdalen's High Table, to the neglect, it seemed of his fellow-Professors in Oxford. Here, burning alive, was that Hohenzollern who had broken in upon the stronghold of the Turk, to snatch the Sultan's standard. Speechless at last, stammering as he subsided, Tolkien glared in outrage at the astonished company. Was this the time or place? Wrenn murmured. Tolkien flung out and came no more to any Conference proceeding.[7]

Tolkien was sceptical of such academic get-togethers, according to Lawlor. In a letter to his son John in 1952, Tolkien made it clear that he thought his friend Wrenn was too attached to academic "politics".

Indeed, Tolkien was an intensely private man, though selectively clubbable. He deeply valued and needed friendship, and he had already found in C.S. Lewis a person worthy of the inner core of the old T.C.B.S. Tolkien was largely responsible at the beginning of the thirties for a dramatic change in the thinking and whole world outlook of his friend, a change that was to lead to the creation of the Inklings, the club of literary friends of central importance to both of them.

Lewis had already moved beyond a bare materialism when he and Tolkien became friends after their initial introduction in 1926 at the English School meeting. After many winding paths, Lewis became a theist, a believer in at least a mind behind the universe, sometime around the end of the twenties. By this time he and Tolkien had discussed many fundamental issues. For Lewis, once a convinced atheist, accepting theism was a huge step. It was not long before he was reading the New Testament (in Greek). The night of 19–20 September 1931, as they made their way down Addison's Walk, in the grounds of Magdalen College, Lewis had a long conversation with Tolkien, and a mutual friend, H.V.D. "Hugo" Dyson, which shook him to the roots. Like Tolkien, Dyson was a devout Christian. Tolkien recorded the long night conversation on Addison's Walk, and many previous exchanges with Lewis, in his poem *Mythopoeia* (the "making of myth"), which he composed a few months or perhaps well over a year later, the first of at least seven versions. He also noted in his diary: "Friendship with Lewis compensates for much, and besides giving constant pleasure and comfort has done me much good from the contact with a man at once honest, brave, intellectual – a scholar, a poet, and a philosopher – and a lover, at least after a long pilgrimage, of Our Lord."[8]

Undoubtedly Dyson gave emotional weight to Tolkien's more measured argument that momentous night. Tolkien had argued for the Christian Gospels on the basis of the universal love of story. *Mythopoeia* (published long after in 1988) gives a good idea of the flow of the conversation. Tolkien wrote of the human heart not being composed of falsehood, but having nourishment of knowledge from the wise God, and still remembering him. Though the estrangement is ancient, human beings are neither completely abandoned by God nor totally corrupted. Though we are disgraced, we still retain vestiges of our mandate to rule. We continue to create according to the "law in which we're made". What convinced Lewis was that the Christian Gospels have all the imaginative pull of pagan myths, with the unique feature of actually describing real happenings in history. There is no separation of tangible events and abstract truth.

Lewis later wrote a powerful essay on the harmony of story and fact in the Gospels, specifically remembering that life-changing conversation with Tolkien and Dyson: "This is the marriage of heaven and earth, perfect Myth and Perfect Fact: claiming not only our love and obedience, but also our wonder and delight, addressed to the savage, the child, and the poet in each one of us no less than to the moralist, the scholar, and the philosopher." He realized that the claims and stories of Christ demanded an imaginative as much as a reasoned response from him.

Tolkien in turn expounded his view more fully in his essay "On Fairy Stories". A form of this was first given as the Andrew Lang Lecture in 1939 at St Andrews University, Scotland (see below). In later, published forms of the essay, he developed his idea that the very events of the Gospel narratives are actual historical events being shaped by God, the master story-maker, having a structure of the sudden turn from catastrophe to the most satisfying of all happy endings – a structure shared with the best human stories. He famously called this kind of happy ending a "eucatastrophe" (a "good catastrophe"). The Gospels, in their divine source, penetrate the seamless "web" of human storytelling, clarifying and perfecting the insights that God in his grace has allowed to the human imagination. In the Gospels, Tolkien concluded, "art has been verified". Among this art, which pointed to the master story of the Gospels, were the northern myths that Tolkien had loved from his boyhood, a love and fascination he shared with Lewis.

As a direct result of Tolkien's argument about myth entering real history, C.S. Lewis began to see a new dimension to his varied group of friends, which was to have a dramatic impact on the very history of English literature, and of theology as well. Groups in Oxford that he had belonged to, some of them with Tolkien, were made up of dons and other academics, such as professors. He now came to value the fact that many of his academic friends, usually friends shared with Tolkien, were professing Christians, albeit of different persuasions – the distinction of Roman Catholic and Protestant being a central one, epitomized in his "Papist" friend, Tolkien, of course. But then there was Owen Barfield, who claimed Christian belief, but it was modified by the mystical teaching of Rudolf Steiner, called Anthroposophy. Furthermore, Barfield was no longer in the academic world, but a family solicitor in the City of London. What he was, however, like many of Lewis's friends, revolved around books and poetry – he was a writer. He could turn his hand to poetry, fiction, and also ground-breaking academic books, like the already published *History in English Words* and *Poetic Diction*. What made up Lewis's friends was therefore quite wide: like Tolkien, they were Christians, they tended to write, and they belonged to more than one profession – they were not all teaching at Oxford. Among his friends, Lewis also counted his brother Warren, fresh from the British Army, who was recently returned to faith, and who was now part of his home on the fringes of Headington, a suburb of Oxford. Through Lewis, Tolkien got to know his brother and to value his friendship, and often got to share a drink with him in one of the plethora of Oxford pubs.

It was this group of friends, less distinct than the academic clusters Tolkien and Lewis frequented, that was the core of what became the Inklings. In an important sense, Tolkien brought the Inklings into existence by persuading Lewis that he needed to commit himself to Christian faith, making this the integration point of his life.

The informal club started around the autumn of 1933, though some believe it might have been a little later than that. For the next sixteen years, on through 1949, the literary friends continued to meet, sometimes in later years in Tolkien's spacious rooms at Merton College after his move from Pembroke College, but more often in Lewis's rooms at Magdalen College, usually on Thursday evenings. By wartime, and possibly before, Tolkien and others had also begun to gather before lunch on Tuesdays, in a snug back room at the Eagle and Child, a public house on St Giles known to locals as "the Bird and Baby".

The Inklings very much embodied the ideals of life and pleasure of Tolkien and Lewis. Tolkien preferred quieter, smaller gatherings; rowdy and boisterous meetings of the Inklings, sometimes associated with a pub venue, were less to his taste – perhaps he was reminded of the T.C.B.S. members who had been purged long before. However, in reality, he was not averse to plunging into the roar of noise emanating from a pub.

In a letter many years later to composer and musician Donald Swann, Tolkien explained that the name "the Inklings" originally belonged to an undergraduate group (of a type common in Oxford in those days). He spoke of reading an early version of his poem "Errantry" to them (later set to music by Swann). The student club, explained Tolkien, used to hear its members read unpublished poems or short tales. The better ones were minuted. The students came up with the name Inklings, and not he or Lewis, who were the only members from the university staff. (Tolkien suspected that they had been invited to give more permanence to the society.) The name was a pun on the fact that its members aspired to write. Tolkien remembered that the club lasted the usual year or two of undergraduate societies. After it folded in the summer term of 1933, its name "became transferred to the circle of C.S. Lewis".

The formation of the Inklings in the autumn term of 1933 (if that indeed was when it started, as is likely) coincided with the natural ending of the Coalbiters, which had by now fulfilled its very specific purpose. Three of the Coalbiters,

Tolkien, Lewis, and Nevill Coghill, were among the new Inklings. C.L. Wrenn helped Tolkien with the teaching of Anglo-Saxon, having joined the university in 1930. Soon after the formation of the Inklings, he was invited to come along. Other early members included Lewis's GP, Dr Robert "Humphrey" Havard, and Lewis's brother, Major Warren Lewis.

We can only speculate about the subjects of conversations, since there is no documentation of the early days. We do know however that chapters of *The Hobbit* were read to the group as it was being finalized for possible publication. We can perhaps glimpse some of the ideas discussed and even celebrated by the Inklings, because Tolkien gave two lectures in the thirties that may have fed into the group. Perhaps the concerns of the Inklings encouraged him to say what he did in these lectures, for in 1936 and 1939 they put forward a number of brilliant and innovative insights. It could be said that the lectures changed the way many people thought about myth, fairy story, and poetry, and even about the relationship of imagination to thought and to language. One of the brilliant but cryptic insights he expressed was: "To ask what is the origins of stories… is to ask what is the origin of language and of the mind."

Tolkien's academic writings, as we have seen, were to become increasingly rare, as his fictional writings took up more of his focus, both as a scholar and a storyteller. One colleague, and a member of the Inklings, who became increasingly concerned about the descent in his writings from the "philological" to the "trivial", especially on the publication of *The Lord of the Rings* in the fifties, was C.L. Wrenn.[9] On 25 November 1936, however, Tolkien gave a lecture to the

British Academy in London. Because of the importance of the occasion Edith accompanied him. Tolkien's title was "Beowulf: The Monsters and the Critics". According to Old English scholar Donald K. Fry, this lecture (published the next year) "completely altered the course of Beowulf studies".[10] It was a defence of the artistic unity of that early English tale. (The oldest surviving manuscript is dated around AD 1000.) Like his later lecture "On Fairy Stories" (1939) and more developed essay (published in 1947), the *Beowulf* lecture and later expanded essay provides an important key to his work both as a scholar and a writer of fiction.

In his lecture, Tolkien expressed dissatisfaction with existing analysis of the *Beowulf* poem. In fact, it had not been done properly, he complained, as it had not been directed to an understanding of the poem as a poem, as a unified work of art. Rather, it had been seen as a quarry for historical information about its period. In particular, the two monsters that dominate it – Grendel, and the dragon – had not been sufficiently considered as the centre and focus of the poem. Tolkien argued that what he called the "structure and conduct" of the poem arose from this central theme of monsters.

It was clear to Tolkien that the *Beowulf* poet created, using great skill, an illusion of historical truth and perspective. Tolkien told his audience that autumn night: "So far from being a poem so poor that only its accidental historical interest can still recommend it, *Beowulf* is in fact so interesting as poetry, in places poetry so powerful, that this quite overshadows the historical content, and is largely independent even of the most important facts... that research has discovered." A literary study of *Beowulf*, Tolkien argued, must deal with a native English poem that is using in a fresh way ancient and mostly traditional material, and thus the focus should not be on the poet's sources, but what he did with them.

Tolkien explained that the poet's choice of the theme of monsters actually accounts for the greatness of the poem. The power comes from "the mythical mode of imagination". Tolkien's approach to *Beowulf* is strikingly true of his own stories:

> The significance of myth is not easily to be pinned on paper by analytical reasoning.... Its defender is thus at a disadvantage: unless he is careful, and speaks in parables, he will kill what he is studying by vivisection, and he will be left with a formal or mechanical allegory... For myth is alive at once and in all its parts, and dies before it can be dissected.

For the writer of *Beowulf*, there is a fusion of the Christian and the ancient north, the old and the new. The author of *Beowulf* explored insights that may be found in the pagan imagination. This is a theme that would be powerfully explored by Tolkien in *The Lord of the Rings*. Indeed most of Tolkien's fiction is set in a pagan, pre-Christian world. Tolkien concluded his lecture by pointing out that:

> In *Beowulf* we have, then, an historical poem about the pagan past, or an attempt at one.... It is a poem by a learned man writing of old times, who looking back on the heroism and sorrow feels in them something permanent and something symbolical. So far from being a confused semi-pagan – historically unlikely for a man

of this sort in the period – he brought probably first to his task a knowledge of Christian poetry....

There are a number of parallels between the author of *Beowulf*, as understood by Tolkien, and Tolkien himself. Tolkien was a Christian storyteller looking back to an imagined northwest European past – his Middle-earth. The *Beowulf* poet was a Christian looking back at the imaginative resources of a pagan past. Both made use of dragons and other potent symbols, symbols that unified their work. Both were concerned more with symbolism than allegory. As with *Beowulf*, what is important is not so much the sources but what was made of them. Like the ancient author, also, Tolkien created an impression of real history and a sense of depths of the past.

In March 1939, over two years later, Tolkien travelled by train up to St Andrews University in Scotland to give the annual Andrew Lang Lecture. His was to be on fairy stories. It set out Tolkien's basic ideas concerning imagination, fantasy, and what he distinctively called "sub-creation". The goal of the lecture was to rehabilitate for adults the idea of the fairy story, which had been relegated to children's literature, and also to rehabilitate fantasy in general. Regarding fairy stories as trivial, suitable only for children, in his view failed to do justice to both fairy stories and real children.

Tolkien, who had by then written much of the basic matter of "The Silmarillion", published *The Hobbit*, and was in the process of writing *The Lord of the Rings*, attempted to set out a structure underlying good fairy tales and fantasies, a structure that would demonstrate that fairy tales were worthy of serious attention.

Fairy tales, he told his audience at St Andrews, were stories about faerie: that is, "the realm or state where fairies have their being". Fairy tales were fantasy, allowing their hearers or readers to move from the details of their limited experience to "survey the depths of space and time". The successful fairy story in fact was "sub-creation", the ultimate achievement of fantasy, the highest art, deriving its power from human language itself. The successful writer of fairy story "makes a Secondary World which your mind can enter. Inside it, what he relates is 'true': it accords with the laws of that world".

In addition to offering a Secondary World, with an "inner consistency of reality", a good fairy tale in Tolkien's view has three other key features. First, it helps to bring about in the reader what he called *recovery* – that is, the restoration of a true view of the meaning of ordinary and humble things that make up human life and reality: things like love, thought, trees, hills, and food. Secondly, the good fairy story offers *escape* from one's narrow and distorted view of reality and meaning. Thirdly, the good fairy story offers *consolation*, leading to joy.

This opportunity to air in public his deepest thoughts about fantasy and fairy tale was an important encouragement to Tolkien – he faced many more years of labour on *The Lord of the Rings*, the "new Hobbit", as his Inklings friends called it. This was a task of composition and incessant revision that had begun in December 1937, months after the publication of *The Hobbit*.

11

Tolkien's second war

It was 14 November 1940, and the war with Germany had been going on for over a year. Tolkien was working late, as was his custom. He began to notice that a strong and strange light was growing and spreading over the northern horizon. Later, he learned that the fiery glow was the burning of Coventry, fifty miles north of Oxford. Many hundreds died in explosions and a firestorm of incendiary bombs that made no distinction between man and woman, child or baby. The heart of the city was destroyed, including the historic cathedral. The Nazis, exultant over the success of this new kind of blitzkrieg using over 500 bombers, invented a word from Coventry's name for the effect on a city of concentrated bombing on this scale – *coventriert* ("Coventrated"). A new phase of mechanized modern conflict had arrived, and its method was used by both foe and friend thereafter. Tolkien was acutely disturbed by modern-style warfare, having experienced it in the Battle of the Somme a quarter of a century before in the use of tanks and saturation shelling of trenches, and now seeing it being espoused on a massively greater scale as a kind of madness in the new conflict in Europe.

Tolkien was doing what he could in his own "war effort", as people called it. He worked extraordinarily hard at extra duties in his senior position at the university as both the student body and the number teaching in the English School became depleted. Just part of his task was to help organize shorter English courses for cadets. Even before the war, when conflict with Hitler was becoming more and more inevitable, he signed up for code-breaking work in the secret service and did some training. He could have ended up in Bletchley Park, where the Nazis' Enigma code was eventually broken by academics, mathematicians, and early computer experts such as Alan Turing. But for some reason it was decided, soon after war started in September 1939, that his cryptographical services were not required. He did, however, become a part-time air-raid warden and member of the Firewatching Service.[1]

Tolkien became used to patrolling leafy streets to the north of Oxford's city centre, observing the changes of the night sky, from cloudy to star-filled. The phases of the moon always greatly interested him, as he noted the changes it made to the ambient light. Walking the Oxford streets in full moonlight was a particular pleasure some on night duty felt, such as his friend C.S. Lewis. Tolkien liked stillness and the absence of traffic, and naturally feared the noise of aircraft in the sky in case any were the enemy. His eyes were used to sweeping buildings for any chinks of light that might be showing. If blackout cover was inadequate, he was ready to swoop.

The cost of a war effort was not merely something he had to bear alone among his family. As war threatened and eventually nightmare became reality, Tolkien was acutely aware of the possible role of his and Edith's children in the conflict. Memories of the previous war were easily revived. John, the eldest, was nearly twenty-two at the outbreak of war, Michael was almost nineteen, Christopher was getting on for fifteen, and Priscilla ten. John's decision to train as a priest would exempt him from call up, but Michael was almost of age, and Christopher would soon be. John was about the same age Tolkien was at the onset of the First World War.

As it turned out, John was nearly caught up in war when he and other trainee priests had to flee to England from his studies in Rome early in 1940 when Mussolini aligned with Hitler. Michael trained as an anti-aircraft gunner (during the Battle of Britain he won the distinguished bravery medal, the George Cross) and then joined the RAF as a gunner on perilous bombing raids over Germany. In 1944 he was invalided out of service and resumed his studies at Oxford. Christopher in turn joined the RAF for pilot training after being allowed to start his studies at Oxford at the age of seventeen in order to get some years of academic work in before his military service. Priscilla was in her school years throughout the war and an important presence in the household, where she at one stage took over some of the typing of her father's *The Lord of the Rings.*

John's return from Italy had a minor part to play in the development of *The Lord of the Rings* as it was being written in drafts and revisions. On his return to England John followed his training college as it was moved first to the Lake District and then to Stonyhurst College in Lancashire. On one occasion, when Tolkien visited Stonyhurst, he and Edith stayed in the small College Lodge, which had some similarities with Gipsy Green, where they had stayed in another wartime. There is a possibility that the name of a local river, the River Shirebourn, in the Shire-like countryside surrounding Stonyhurst College, suggested the River Shirebourn in Tolkien's Shire in the story.

Christopher's service in the RAF also had a part in Tolkien's writing, but in a different way. When he joined the Royal Air Force in 1942, Christopher was soon dispatched to South Africa for his training as a fighter pilot. While Christopher was there, Tolkien sent him long letters reporting the progress of *The Lord of the Rings*, and providing glimpses of his meetings with Lewis, Charles Williams, and the Inklings. Williams had been introduced to the group before the war. When Oxford University Press staff were evacuated from London to Oxford at the onset of war, he became an active and regular member of the Inklings.

This frequent correspondence was an important impetus to his father. Christopher, more than any of the Tolkien children, had been closely involved with the creation of the story since its beginning, and in 1943 he made for his father a large and elaborate map of Middle-earth in pencil and coloured chalks, closely based upon Tolkien's primitive but precise maps. These grew from the original sketching of the Shire in 1938. Christopher shared a special affinity with his father, which may be reflected in the father–son relationships in the unfinished story "The Lost Road" of a few years before. This affinity gave Christopher a natural facility in untangling and making sense of the numerous drafts of "The Silmarillion" Tolkien left upon his death.

Family matters aside, Tolkien struggled with the burden of increased academic duties as Rawlinson and Bosworth Professor of Anglo-Saxon, including administrative tasks in the English School. His letters are full of references to committee and council meetings, and the care of individual research students and the needs of cadet students. He suffered broken and often sleepless nights as a result of his duties as an air-raid warden, which seem to have lasted from sometime in autumn 1940 to the end of the requirement of blackouts around September 1944. During most of this gruelling regime he was able to find time frequently to meet up with C.S. Lewis, often with his brother Warren (and sometimes with Charles Williams also in attendance), or for meetings with the larger group of Inklings. The group's gatherings could go on to midnight or beyond, unless Tolkien or Lewis or others were on duty and had to leave earlier (Lewis was in the Home Guard). Apart from a gap of about a year, and some smaller periods when creativity seemed to dissipate, Tolkien wrote much of *The Lord of the Rings* in the war years, reading chapters as they were written to some members or to the Inklings group. All provided the encouragement Tolkien sometimes desperately needed.

With all these efforts Tolkien conscientiously fulfilled his role, as he saw it, in the household. Many a morning or afternoon might be taken up, in part or whole, with mending or building a henhouse or chicken run, as the garden was gradually transformed to a wartime footing, providing fresh eggs and vegetables to help feed the family. (Edith's aviary provided the basis of the hen house.[2]) In 1930, upon moving to 20 Northmoor Road, Tolkien, with the help of his sons, had dug up a tennis court to make a vegetable garden. This proved to be a boon in the wartime. Health and education bills were a constant demand, and Tolkien as the sole wage earner was often broke. He would write to his publisher for advance payment of royalties or to chase late payments. He, like many of his colleagues, continued to experience long hours of tedium marking school examination papers in the summer vacations for some extra money. The family at one stage accommodated a couple of women evacuees from London. These evacuees missed London and their husbands so much that they returned there after some months despite the risk of bombs.

The family would gather around the large Pye radio to listen intently to news bulletins from the BBC. They also heard the sneering voice of "Lord Haw-Haw", the traitor William Joyce, broadcasting from Germany. Priscilla Tolkien got used to the frequent tapping from upstairs of her father's heavy and ancient Hammond typewriter, as he keyed his way through successive drafts of his emerging *The Lord of the Rings*. Oxford's University Examination Schools were turned into a military hospital. Tolkien's College, Pembroke, was partially requisitioned by the Ministry of Agriculture as well as the army. At lunch one day Tolkien, with a chuckle, told the family that a notice had appeared in the College Lodge. It announced, "*Pests: First Floor.*"

Tolkien and Edith celebrated their silver wedding anniversary in 1941, necessarily a modest occasion due to the limitations created by the war. Of the children, only Priscilla could attend, but guests included Hugo Dyson and C.S. Lewis. Edith suffered frequent bouts of ill health throughout the war years, and still had little engagement in Tolkien's working life. Lewis was often puzzled by complicated afflictions Tolkien seemed to bear in his married life. If Edith was away (perhaps because of a spell in hospital), Lewis would sometimes be invited to Northmoor Road for what he once called "the old, old talk" or to hear another episode from *The Lord of the Rings*.

Despite the disruptions of war, including a shortage of students, the university carried on as normally as possible. Tolkien and Lewis continued to lecture, Tolkien oversaw his graduate students, and Lewis held his morning and early evening tutorials for undergraduates. Charles Williams had published inspiring literary criticism such as *Reason and Beauty in the Poetic Mind* (1933) and was an expert on the poetry of Dante. It became obvious to Tolkien and C.S. Lewis that he had an extraordinary knowledge of English literature. They recruited him to augment the teaching of the understaffed English School with his wide knowledge of poetry, and his lectures were very popular with students. He did this lecturing on top of his normal duties as part of the editorial staff of Oxford University Press. After he had spoken to a surprised audience of students on the theme of virginity in John Milton's *Comus,* Dyson joked that Williams was in danger of becoming a thoroughgoing "chastitute". On one occasion in 1943 Tolkien and Williams found themselves lecturing at the very same time. Whereas Williams's lecture on *Hamlet* filled the auditorium, Tolkien's students all but deserted him to hear Williams. So Tolkien was left to lecture on Anglo-Saxon to a solitary student. Unperturbed, he had a drink with Williams afterwards.

Late in life, Tolkien implied in several letters that he and Williams had little in common in their writings and thinking. In contrast, however, Williams's move to Oxford at the beginning of the war, and his admittance into the Inklings, helped to exert a deep and lasting influence on Lewis, particularly in the way Williams drew theology out of intense human experiences such as falling in love. Tolkien in later years described Lewis as being under Williams's "spell", and did not entirely approve of this, feeling that Lewis was too impressionable a man. Later also, he would refer to the Inklings as Lewis's "séance", alluding to Williams's fascination with the occult, a taste that disturbed Tolkien. The true picture is that, at the time, Tolkien got a lot out of his friendship with Williams, and deeply appreciated his attentive listening to episodes of *The Lord of the Rings* as they were written.

Tolkien would listen carefully to Williams reading from his fiction, poetry, or other work, even though he confessed that, at times, he found Williams's work difficult to make out. Lewis described one such occasion when Williams read a piece of his that was more to Tolkien's liking, *The Figure of Arthur,* Williams's unfinished prose study of the Arthurian legend.

> Picture to yourself... an upstairs sitting-room with windows looking north into the "grove" of Magdalen College on a sunshiny Monday Morning in vacation at about ten o'clock. The Professor and I, both on the Chesterfield, lit our pipes and stretched out our legs. Williams in the arm-chair opposite to us threw his cigarette into the grate, took up a pile of the extremely small, loose sheets on which he habitually wrote – they came, I think, from a twopenny pad for memoranda, and began [reading]....[3]

Charles Williams was an evacuee of sorts, with his wife Florence remaining in London to look after their flat. Fifty employees of the London office of Oxford University Press were moved to Oxford. It was two weeks before Williams's fifty-third birthday. He was billeted at 9 South Parks Road, a few minutes' walk from the city centre. This was home to Professor H.N. Spalding, who founded the Chair of Eastern Religion and Ethics at Oxford, and his family. Williams settled into the domestic establishment quickly. Soon he was cutting bread for everyone at meals, even though his hands habitually shook, opening windows to air the rooms, and drying dishes. William Wordsworth or Milton were likely to be quoted in eloquent draughts in his conversation, and the topic might range anywhere from earth to heaven. T.S. Eliot, his publisher and a great admirer of his writings, said:

> For him there was no frontier between the material and the spiritual world. Had I ever to spend a night in a haunted house, I should have felt secure with Williams in my company: he was somehow protected from evil, and was himself a protection... The deeper things are there just because they belonged to the world he lived in, and he could not have kept them out.[4]

Williams regularly met up with Lewis and Tolkien, and attended the Inklings, which established two meetings a week after war broke: Tuesday mornings in a pub like the Eagle and Child in St Giles and Thursday (or sometimes Friday) evenings in Lewis's, and occasionally Tolkien's, college rooms. This new arrangement of the two types of gatherings reflected the growth of the group and a heightened fervency to their gatherings. The largely self-educated Williams spoke with a marked East London accent, which was unusual to the ears of university academics, who were usually public school educated (Tolkien was an exception, with his grammar school background). The distinguished theologian E.L. Mascall remembered Williams, though a small man, for "the excitability and volubility of his speech" through which "his enormous interior energy and enthusiasm was manifested and became infectious".

Though Williams won a place at University College London, beginning as a student there at the age of fifteen, the fees proved too much for his family, and Williams was forced to discontinue his studies. His fortunes changed through meeting an editor from the London office of the Oxford University Press, who was looking for help with the proofs of an edition of the complete works of the Victorian novelist William Makepeace Thackeray. Williams would remain with the OUP until his death, creating a distinctive atmosphere remembered with affection by those who worked with him, particularly women. He married Florence Conway, whom he called "Michal" after King David's wife in the Bible who scorned the king's dancing. In the First World War Williams was considered medically unfit to serve and, like Tolkien, lost two of his closest friends in the trenches.

Williams spent the years from 1939 until 1945 in Oxford. They involved his normal editorial duties with Oxford University Press, lecturing and tutorials for the university, regular gatherings with individual Inklings friends as well as the group, and occasional weekends with Florence back in London, a city he loved. Williams played an integral role in the war years of the Inklings, years that were part of their golden age. Themes central to his imagination and writing, including the reality of the supernatural world, heaven, and hell, were also dominant themes in the writings of Tolkien and C.S. Lewis in these years. In Tolkien they were less explicit than in Lewis, but *The Lord of the Rings* is dominated by the devilry of Sauron, the Dark Lord, and the bright hope of the Undying Lands over the seas in the distant West. C.S. Lewis dedicated one of his most popular books, *The Screwtape Letters,* to Tolkien. The letters, from a senior to a junior devil, had been read in weekly episodes to the Inklings, to explosions of laughter and their constant amusement.

Though he was somewhat bemused by the dedication, Tolkien's letters at the time frequently reflect concepts, often moral ones, explored in *Screwtape*. In just the same way he used the idea of Lewis's *hnau* (personal beings with personal, "human" qualities being embodied in animal or vegetable form) from his science fiction stories. He did this in reflecting upon some developments in the narrative of *The Lord of the Rings*. Lewis's idea may have influenced Tolkien's notion of Ents, where trees are sentient and have personality, including speech, and the creation of Treebeard. Treebeard the Ent was the oldest and most venerable of the tree-creatures, and one of the oldest living beings in Middle-earth at the time of *The Lord of the Rings.*

Sometimes in the uncertain war years progress halted on the writing of *The Lord of the Rings*. During one such hiatus was born an intensely personal story. It was inspired by a neighbour's threat to chop down a poplar tree in the street outside his home. *Leaf by Niggle* was a tale of hope and spiritual growth involving the idea of a Purgatory – a state between hell and heaven.

Leaf by Niggle was published in January 1945 in *The Dublin Review*, but written some time before. Niggle, a little man and an artist, knew that he would one day have to make a journey. Many matters got in the way of his painting, such as the demands of his neighbour, Mr Parish, who had a lame leg. Niggle was somewhat lazy, and rather soft-hearted. He was concerned to finish one painting in particular. This had started as an illustration of a leaf caught in the wind, then the work kept developing until it became a whole tree. Through gaps in the leaves and branches a forest and a whole world opened up.

The journey Niggle had to make was death. Many years later Tolkien pointed out that a central theme of *The Lord of the Rings* also concerns death. After a period in the Work House (Purgatory), Niggle was allowed to resume his journey in a small train that led him to the world depicted in his painting of long ago, and to his tree, now perfectly and gloriously complete.

Long before, back in the town near where Niggle and Parish had lived before the journey, a fragment of Niggle's painting had survived and been hung in the town museum, entitled simply, "Leaf by Niggle". It depicted a spray of leaves with a glimpse of a mountain peak. Niggle's Country became a popular place to send travellers to for a holiday, for refreshment and convalescence, and as a splendid introduction to the mountains.

Tolkien's little story suggests the link between reality and art. There will be room for the artist to add his or her own touch to the created world even in heaven. Niggle the painter stands for Tolkien the fastidious writer. The way he paints leaves rather than trees reflects Tolkien's perfectionism, and his propensity to be easily distracted. Niggle's leaf may be the equivalent of Tolkien's *The Hobbit*. If this is so, it would follow that Niggle's tree resembles the large undertakings of *The Lord of the Rings* and the vast background work of "The Silmarillion".

After completing *Leaf by Niggle*, Tolkien was once again able to resume his work on *The Lord of the Rings*. He saw the mythology that he was creating in his Middle-earth as his "own internal Tree".[5] He continued to be encouraged by the responses of C.S. Lewis and Charles Williams to his readings of chapters in progress, and also to the reception he received to the readings from the larger Inklings group.

The Inklings continued throughout the war years with their familiar pattern of the two types of meetings: the literary gatherings usually in Lewis's rooms in Magdalen College (or sometimes in Tolkien's in Pembroke or, later, in Merton College after he moved there), and the more informal meetings in the Eagle and Child pub or, occasionally, similar haunts. In better times, they had taken walking tours together. Lewis wrote: "My happiest hours are spent with three or four old friends in old clothes tramping together and putting up in small pubs – or else sitting up till the small hours in someone's college rooms talking nonsense, poetry, theology, metaphysics over beer, tea and pipes."

Lewis gives the flavour of a typical Thursday night literary meeting in a letter to his brother in November 1939. "On Thursday we had a meeting of the Inklings ... we dined at the Eastgate [Hotel]. I have never in my life seen Dyson so exuberant – 'A roaring cataract of nonsense'. The bill of fare afterwards consisted of a section of the new Hobbit book from Tolkien, a nativity play from Williams (unusually intelligible for him, and approved by all), and a chapter out of the book on the Problem of Pain from me." The piece read by Tolkien at this time may have been a reworked section of Book One of *The Fellowship of the Ring* – he was making momentous changes relating, among other things, to the nature of the Ring "to rule them all" and to the identity of Aragorn, the future king. Whatever the piece it must have touched upon the nature of evil, as Lewis remarks later in his letter that the subject matter of the readings that evening "formed almost a logical sequence". Evil that bedevils so much of human life was a dominant theme both of Williams's play, *The House by the Stable,* and Lewis's *The Problem of Pain.*

According to a one-time member of the group, the novelist and poet John Wain, after Charles Williams's sudden death in 1945, which was a grievous blow to the Inklings, the two most active members became once more Tolkien and Lewis. Wain writes: "While C.S. Lewis attacked [the whole current of contemporary art and life] on a wide front, with broadcasts, popular-theological books, children's stories, romances, and controversial literary criticism, Tolkien concentrated on the writing of his colossal 'Lord of the Rings' trilogy. His readings of each successive installment were eagerly received...." In 1949, when the book was completed bar minor changes, Lewis was lent the typescript. He responded: "I have drained the rich cup and satisfied a long thirst.... All the long years you have spent on it are justified."

Central to *The Lord of the Rings* is the war against Sauron and his enslavement fought by the free peoples of the West. The Ring is essentially a machine made by the Dark Lord's technological skill, Tolkien explained. As an object it holds Sauron's power, which he deliberately puts into it. Effectively, he places his heart and soul in it. With its destruction he becomes a powerless wraith. The war of the Ring is between those who would wield the Ring for power and those who reject its use, for the end of its use is always enslavement, no matter how good the intentions of the user. Though the main sources of Tolkien's portrayal of the battle between good and evil in Middle-earth lie in his experiences and perception of the First World War, he was aware of the applicability of his story to the Second World War. This was not however a simple allegory, such as the Ring representing the atomic bomb, as some interpreted it. Rather, Tolkien saw the Second World War, like the battle of the Ring, as a war of the machine. He wrote to his son Christopher, in far-off South Africa, that this was "the first War of the Machines".[6] He also said of the war, in another letter, "We are attempting to conquer Sauron with the Ring. And we shall (it seems) succeed. But the penalty is, you will know, to breed new Saurons, and slowly turn Men and Elves into Orcs."[7]

12

The struggle to publish

Although Tolkien finished writing a reasonably complete version of *The Lord of the Rings* by 1949, the first two volumes would not be published until five years later, with *The Return of the King* appearing the following year. Even to get to this stage of writing had meant overcoming many obstacles, both personal and work related. (Even his dealings with his publisher and another potential publisher could fill a small book.) The Inklings, especially C.S. Lewis, provided valuable and much-needed encouragement as he struggled to finish *The Lord of the Rings*.

The support given by the Inklings as a group, however, began to fade away when, around the spring of 1947, Hugo Dyson started exercising a veto against the reading of further instalments (though Tolkien continued to read when Dyson was absent). Dyson was tired of constantly hearing about Elves. Clearly, he had lost interest in, and was not really in sympathy with, Tolkien's unfolding epic, unlike Lewis, Charles Williams in the war years, Warren Lewis, and probably other Inklings (unless some kept a polite silence). Less than three years after Hugo Dyson began to veto Tolkien's reading, the literary meetings of the group – where work in progress was read out to the group – foundered and may have even stopped altogether. Warren Lewis records one such silencing of Tolkien in his diary: "A well attended Inkling this evening – both the Tolkiens [father and son, Christopher], J[ack] and I, Humphrey [Havard], Gervase [Mathew], Hugo; the latter came in just as we were starting on the '[new] Hobbit', and as he now exercises a veto in it – most unfairly I think – we had to stop." Father Gervase Mathew, a Dominican priest and lecturer at Oxford, had joined the Inklings not long before.

Often without the chance to read his instalments to the Inklings, Tolkien needed the encouragement of C.S. Lewis more than ever to complete the writing of *The Lord of the Rings*. On occasions he read to Lewis and Warren Lewis, or just Lewis (whose appetite for tales of Elves was inexhaustible), outside of the "official" Inklings meetings. There was never enough dissent, however, to weaken Tolkien's appreciation of the Inklings for the long years they had listened and responded to chapters in progress: when *The Fellowship of the Ring* appeared in 1954, it carried a dedication to his friends, the Inklings, in its foreword. He explained the dedication as being "because they have already listened to it with a patience, and indeed with an interest, that almost leads me to suspect that they have hobbit-blood in their venerable ancestry".[1]

One event that figured strongly in demands on his writing time for *The Lord of the Rings* was his change of Chairs at Oxford in 1945. This also marked big changes in his family life. He moved to the Merton Chair of English Language and Literature, after having been Bosworth and Rawlinson Professor of Anglo-Saxon since coming south from Leeds in

1925, twenty years before. This new Chair involved special responsibility for Middle English up to AD 1500 (which was roughly the date after which he thought that there was no point in teaching any English literature – unlike C.S. Lewis, whose break-off point was around 1830). The move reflected his wider interests, particularly the language and literature of the West Midlands, for which he felt a strong affinity, because of his roots in "the Shire". With the new professorship, as was the custom, he became a fellow of its associated college, Merton. Tolkien soon settled into his college and when later in the year a second Merton English Chair became vacant, his immediate wish was that it would go to Lewis. "It ought to be C.S. Lewis," he wrote at the time, "or perhaps Lord David Cecil, but one never knows." Tolkien, as an Elector for the Chair, had a considerable sway, but despite his vote, his friend was passed over in favour of F.P. Wilson, a former English tutor of Lewis's when Lewis was an undergraduate. Tolkien was delighted, however, eventually to have two Inklings, Hugo Dyson and Nevill Coghill, join the fellows at Merton College. Dyson became fellow and tutor in English Literature at Merton in 1945, and Coghill joined the college in 1957, upon becoming Merton Professor of English Literature. Tolkien's delight over Dyson's appointment was tempered somewhat, however, by the fact that his friend was given the college rooms that overlooked the meadows that he had hoped to have!

Merton owned houses rented by its staff, which at times became available. Tolkien put his name down for one. A house became free in 1947, 3 Manor Road, not far by foot from Merton College. It was a small, brick house – how small was not appreciated until he, Edith, and Priscilla moved into it. Edith and he reluctantly had decided that 20 Northmoor Road was too big for their needs now that John, Michael, and Christopher were no longer at home; the cost of maintaining it could not be tolerated. Michael was married, with a young son, and teaching at the Oratory School, south of Wallingford, Oxfordshire; John was serving as a priest in Coventry; Christopher was in digs in Oxford, studying at Trinity College; and Priscilla was still at school. At Manor Road, Tolkien had no study; he was forced to use an attic bedroom. Much of the final stages of *The Lord of the Rings* was typed here with two fingers, Tolkien's typewriter sitting on the bed. There was nothing for it but to wait for another Merton house to come up.

Eventually an old house in an attractive row became available, 99 Holywell Street. It had steps up to the front door, and even its small garden was not claustrophobic like the one in Manor Road had been. A happy hawthorn tree grew there, and on the other side of the high back wall (a section of Oxford's medieval wall) were the gardens of New College. Blackwell's Bookshop lay just down the street towards the city centre, into Broad Street, as well as the Kings Arms pub (sometimes frequented by the Inklings), and the Bodleian Library, containing most of the books ever published in Britain, and much more to delight Tolkien's heart. Close by the house, around the corner in Longwall Street, was the site of the first Morris garage, opened by William Morris in 1902 to repair and service cars, before he started making them in 1912. The location is somewhat ironic, given Tolkien's abandonment of car use some years before their move to Holywell Street, and his occasional mutterings about "Mordor in our midst" at the noise and clutter of industrial life long before the public had heard about Sauron's stronghold.

During the immediate post-war years and into the fifties, Edith remained quite isolated from Tolkien's Oxford life. There had been times when B.Litt. students would stay with the family, and some turned into permanent friends. She also became friends with the occasional colleague of her husband: in the case of C.L. Wrenn, she developed a strong friendship with his wife Agnes. Edith also kept in touch with Mabel Sheaf, a friend she had made at Dresden House School, in Evesham, before she met the young Tolkien in Birmingham. She was sorry to be parted from her when she and her family emigrated to New Zealand after the war. There were public occasions, too, at the university, to which Mrs Tolkien was invited. It is quite likely that Edith attended a particularly memorable one on 25 May 1948. When the young Princess Elizabeth was presented with an honorary degree of Doctor of Civil Law at the Sheldonian Theatre, over one and a half thousand guests afterwards attended a garden party for her. During the celebrations, Her Majesty watched a special masque created in her honour and performed by the university dramatic society, together with a white horse.[2] Sadly, Edith would not live to see Elizabeth, then Queen, present Tolkien with a CBE (Commander of the Order of the British Empire) for services to English literature nearly a quarter of a century later.

After some years in Holywell Street, in March 1953 Tolkien and Edith moved to 76 Sandfield Road in Oxford's suburb of Headington. Priscilla had left home in 1950, to study at Bristol University. She eventually became a probation officer. Wartime austerity continued for a number of years after the conflict ended. Some American admirers were in the much-appreciated habit of sending food parcels to C.S. Lewis, who had become something of a celebrity after having appeared on the cover of *Time* magazine, 8 September 1947 issue. Edith was frequently ill, sometimes seriously. One time, receiving such a parcel, and having heard that Edith was unwell, Lewis passed it on to the Tolkien household without opening it. He soon had to go back to reclaim some stationery printed with his details that, unaware to him, had been included in with the consumables. Every now and then Lewis was able to host a "ham supper" or similar for the Inklings, to share the benefice of such food parcels.

For complex reasons, the friendship between Tolkien and C.S. Lewis cooled somewhat, starting in the war years, though this chilling has sometimes been exaggerated. In fact, the strong friendship never died, but had its ups and downs, perhaps a little like Tolkien's emotional life, scarred by the First World War. The arrival of Charles Williams in Oxford may have been a factor. As Tolkien's friendship with Lewis deepened not very long after their meeting in 1926, it had become rather like the intimacy shared years before by the inner core of the old T.C.B.S. Similarly, Lewis grew to see it as a first order one, like his friendship with his Belfast soul mate, Arthur Greeves. In a strange sense, there was perhaps some jealousy of Williams on Tolkien's part as he saw Lewis becoming so friendly with him, maybe borne out of past loss and insecurity.

The sudden death of Charles Williams in May 1945 had not fully restored the old intimacy; while Tolkien felt Williams's loss keenly, he still considered Lewis was too taken with him. The continuing influence of Williams on Lewis after his death, reinforced by Tolkien's dislike of Lewis's popular theology, cast something of a shadow between them. Tolkien felt that theology should be communicated by those properly qualified, rather than by a layperson like Lewis. He himself preferred his Christian faith to be implicit and allusive in his work, though he took great pains to ensure that his fictional creation of Middle-earth, including its cosmology, was in harmony with core Christian belief. This is not to say that there are no allusions to denominational Roman Catholic belief in his fiction. Tolkien himself described *The Lord of the Rings* as a "fundamentally religious and Catholic work".[3]

With the temperature of the friendship having dropped, perhaps imperceptibly, Tolkien may have found it harder than usual to accept Lewis's well-meant criticisms of *The Lord of the Rings* in some places, despite the enormous encouragement his friend exercised. This however did not weaken Tolkien's resolve to place his friend in a Chair. It was quite absurd that a teacher and scholar such as Lewis, who stood out even in a centre of learning like Oxford, did not already have a professorship. If it wasn't to be the Merton professorship, then it would be another. Though he considered Lewis's popularizing of theology a flaw in his friend's output, he did not sympathize with a general hostility to Lewis in the Oxford hierarchy, reflected in passing over his friend for the Merton Chair and perhaps in a later failure to give him the Professorship of Poetry in 1951. In fact, he was grateful to Lewis as a close ally in the reforms he had accomplished in the syllabus of the Oxford English School.

The Lord of the Rings drew near to its completion, with only the extensive appendices remaining and matters of consistency to be reconciled. (It had taken him a long time to sort out the phases of the moon in the interlacing stories, for instance.) Tolkien thought back to that time in a BBC radio interview: "I remember I actually wept at the denouement. But then of course there was a tremendous lot of revision. I typed the whole of that work out twice and lots of it many times, on a bed in an attic [in Manor Road]. I couldn't afford of course the typing."[4] Some of the final writing and revision for consistency was accomplished in the tranquillity of the Oratory School near Wallingford, where his son Michael taught, which had moved from its original location in the Birmingham Oratory. Tolkien stayed there in a master's room for much of the long vacation in the summer of 1949. It was a fitting environment for his task as, of course, part of his childhood had been spent in the vicinity of the Birmingham Oratory School.

In those post-war years, publishing in Britain was accomplished by outstanding independent houses like George Allen and Unwin (which had brought out *The Hobbit*), William Collins, and Faber & Faber. Some were quite small, but nevertheless distinctive, like C.S. Lewis's publisher, Geoffrey Bles. The industry was very different from that of today, dominated as it is by multinational corporations. The truth is that the publication of *The Lord of the Rings* only took place because of the combined flair of Tolkien's then publisher, and its willingness to take on what it considered to be a loss maker – ironically, in upfront costing, Tolkien's trilogy was allowed to be carried by other books seen as successful. Despite daunting obstacles, the publishing climate at that time may have been the most conducive ever for Tolkien's epic fantasy to be published. It could easily have remained a story known only to a few friends and family, even with the earlier success of *The Hobbit*. For one thing, *The Hobbit* was clearly a children's book, and at that time fantasy was perceived as something for the little ones. *The Lord of the Rings* was not a children's book, and did not fit any of the well-worn readerships identified by publishers of the time.

As it turned out, publication by George Allen and Unwin was to be delayed for a number of years for reasons very much to do with the arcane practices of publishers, even a top rate house like that. The biggest reason for the long delay, however, was Tolkien's unrealistic wish to publish the still unfinished "The Silmarillion" at the same time as *The Lord of the Rings*. Raynor Unwin, who had read the typescript of *The Hobbit* as a child for his father's company, had shown an unambiguous interest in early drafts of part of the "new Hobbit". Indeed, in July 1947, when Tolkien dropped off a section of the first book at George Allen and Unwin's offices near the British Museum in London, Raynor put everything aside to read through it and to provide a report. His father also had strongly and consistently encouraged Tolkien to produce a sequel to *The Hobbit*. Despite this, Tolkien wrongly understood as rejection or coolness the publisher's hesitations over "The Silmarillion" material, which was totally unlike the unfolding, and itself problematic, *The Lord of the Rings*. Tolkien made up his mind that both "The Silmarillion" and *The Lord of the Rings* must be published together. He also mistakenly computed that both would be around the same length, adding to the disquiet of his publisher.

Late in 1949, with joint publication in mind, Tolkien sent Milton Waldman, a commissioning editor at another quality publisher, William Collins, the large typescript of *The Lord of the Rings*. In February the next year Waldman expressed an interest in "The Silmarillion", but later Collins changed its mind when the full implications of trying to publish the category-defying work became clearer. One consideration for all publishers at this time of post-war reconstruction and austerity was paper costs and shortages. Perhaps the only benefit of this unfortunate delay was that in 1951 Tolkien wrote a 10,000-word letter to Waldman explaining "The Silmarillion", a document that is one of the best keys to the extraordinary legendarium (as Tolkien called it) outside of the published, condensed *The Silmarillion* in 1977. Eventually, on 22 June 1952 Tolkien offered *The Lord of the Rings* unconditionally to George Allen and Unwin – who were still enthusiastic and sent Raynor Unwin to Oxford to pick up the original, and only, manuscript on 9 September 1952. Because of its length, the publisher decided to publish the work in three parts. The first two volumes – *The Fellowship of the Ring* and *The Two Towers* – came out on 29 July 1954 and 11 November 1954, respectively, with the final volume – *The Return of the King* – appearing the next year, on 20 October 1955. Readers therefore had to wait nearly a year to find out what happened to Frodo the Hobbit, captured by orcs on the borders of Mordor. Tolkien admitted to Sir Stanley Unwin how much he had given of himself in writing *The Lord of the Rings*. "It is," he said, "written in my life-blood, such as that is, thick or thin; and I can no other."[5]

In November 1952 Tolkien had signed a contract with George Allen and Unwin that specified a share in any profits from the book, rather than the usual percentage royalty of sales. This was because the publisher expected the ambitious publication to make a loss. It turned out that Tolkien would eventually earn vastly more than if he had had the usual royalty payments!

That summer, Tolkien had taken a holiday in the town of Malvern, in Worcestershire, with his friend George Sayer, who was the English master at Malvern College. To divert him in the evening, Sayer pulled out a bulky open-reel tape recorder. The machine was new to Tolkien. To cast out any demon that might be lurking in it, he asked if he could record the Lord's Prayer in the ancient Gothic language he loved. When he heard the result, he was delighted and asked if he might record some of the poems from *The Lord of the Rings*. The more he recorded, which included some of the narrative, the more his confidence grew. The experience appealed to his theatrical side. Sayer remembered that

> it was easy to entertain [Tolkien] by day. He and
> I tramped the Malvern Hills which he had often
> seen during his boyhood in Birmingham or from his
> brother's house on the other side of the Severn River
> valley. He lived the book as we walked, sometimes
> comparing parts of the hills with, for instance, the
> White Mountains of Gondor. We drove to the Black
> Mountains on the borders of Wales, picked bilberries
> and climbed through the heather there. We picnicked
> on bread and cheese and apples, and washed them
> down with perry, beer or cider. When we saw signs of
> industrial pollution, he talked of orcs and orcery. At
> home he helped me to garden. Characteristically what
> he liked most was to cultivate a very small area, say a
> square yard, extremely well.[6]

George Sayer had met Tolkien five years before in Malvern, in August 1947, when he joined Lewis and his brother Warren.

The brothers liked to hike on the hills and had persuaded "Tollers" (as they sometimes called him) on that occasion to join them, even if it was only for part of their holiday. Tolkien, they found, tended to amble, taking in the details of the countryside, whereas the others wished to press on. Warren recorded in his diary:

Tollers fitted easily into our routine, and I think he enjoyed himself. His one fault turned out to be that he wouldn't trot at our pace in harness; he will keep on going all day on a walk, but to him, with his botanical and entomological interests, a walk, no matter what its lengths, is what we would call an extended stroll, while he calls us "ruthless walkers". However, we managed two good days with him including one to the top of the [British] Camp... On this day we had the company of George Sayer... Our nice bar lady has left... and been replaced by a sulky Glaswegian with a patch of plaster in his forehead, who was truculent at our disapproval of his abominable beer: as Tollers said after the encounter, it was easy to see how he came by the patch!... He... had drunk with us at the excellent pub, the Unicorn: of which he heartily approved: and his visit added a private piece of nomenclature to Malvern – the christening of the mysterious and ornate little green and silver doors in the wall of the old cab rank in Pring Rd [sic] as "Sackville Baggins's".[7]

Warren Lewis naturally understood Tolkien's reference to the house of the greedy Hobbit family, having heard much of *The Lord of the Rings* read out by then.

C.S. Lewis reviewed *The Fellowship of the Ring* enthusiastically in *Time & Tide,* a literary and political magazine to which he often contributed. The review opened, "This book is like lightning from a clear sky." It was, Lewis added, "the conquest of new territory".

Response to *The Lord of the Rings* tended to polarize. As a work of literature, the strengths and weaknesses of *The Lord of the Rings* have been extensively discussed by scholars and countless readers and continue to this day to divide the critics. Among its admirers was W.H. Auden. In his *New York Times* review of *The Return of the King* on 22 January 1956, he writes:

> I rarely remember a book about which I have had such violent arguments. Nobody *seems* to have a moderate opinion: either, like myself, people find it a masterpiece of its genre or they cannot abide it, and among the hostile there are some, I must confess, for whose literary judgment I have great respect... I can only suppose that some people object to Heroic Quests and Imaginary Worlds on principle; such, they feel, cannot be anything but light "escapist" reading. That a man like Mr. Tolkien, the English philologist who teaches at Oxford, should lavish such incredible pains upon a genre which is, for them, trifling by definition, is, therefore, very shocking.

Some readers enjoy the "Hobbitry" of the early chapters. Many who do not, but persevere in the reading, find the tone and mood change as the journey of the Ring-bearer increasingly grips the imagination. The Shire, from whence Frodo sets off with Sam and other friends, and to which he returns, in fact represents the ordinary human world. All the dangers that are faced on the perilous journey have meaning because such an ordinary world has to be able to exist, or all is lost.

One mark of the quality of *The Lord of the Rings* as literature is its basis in language. Tolkien makes use of his invented languages in names, and also in imaginative possibility. Language is the basis of the background mythology. Another mark of its literary quality is Tolkien's success in integrating the wealth of symbolism in his story. Quest, the journey, sacrifice, healing, death, and many other symbolic elements are beautifully developed in the book. The very landscapes through which the travellers pass are symbolic, suggesting moods that correspond to the stage of the journey, and to the phase of the overall story. The terrors of Moria, the archetypal underworld, for example, contrast with the spiritual refreshment of Lórien. Always, these landscapes are fully part of the movement of the story throughout the book.

The Lord of the Rings is a heroic romance, telling of the quest to destroy the one, ruling Ring of power, before it can fall into the hands of its maker, Sauron, the Dark Lord of the book's title. As a consistent, unified story, it stands independently of the invented mythology and historical chronicles of Middle-earth recorded in "The Silmarillion". Events of the past provide a backdrop and haunting dimension to the story.

Briefly, the basic storyline of *The Lord of the Rings* begins as Gandalf, the Wizard, discovers that the Ring found by the Hobbit Bilbo (as told in *The Hobbit*) is in fact the One Ring, controlling the Rings of Power forged in the Second Age in Eregion, a region of Middle-earth lying on the western side of the Misty Mountains. Frodo, who inherits the Ring from his uncle Bilbo, flees from the comfort of the Shire with his companions. On his trail are the Black Riders, sent from the evil realm of Mordor by Sauron. With the help of the Ranger, Aragorn, they succeed in reaching the security of Rivendell, one of the few Elven kingdoms remaining in Middle-earth. There, Elrond of Rivendell holds a great Council where it is decided that the Ring must be destroyed, and that Frodo should be the Ring-bearer. The Company of the Ring is also chosen to help him on the desperate quest. Led by Gandalf, they are the four Hobbits Frodo, Sam, Merry, and Pippin, the men Aragorn and Boromir, the Elf Legolas, and the Dwarf Gimli. The Ring can only be destroyed in the Mountain of Fire, Mount Doom, in Mordor.

Frustrated in their attempt to cross the Misty Mountains in the snow, the Company is led by Gandalf into the underground mines of Moria, once worked by Dwarves. Here dwells a dreadful Balrog, a spirit of the underworld from the dawn of creation. Gandalf, in great sacrifice, gives his life fighting the evil spirit to allow the others to escape. The Company is led on by Aragorn, revealed as the secret heir of the ancient Kings of the West. They pass through the blessed Elven realm of Lórien and then down the great River Anduin. The creature Gollum – encountered by Bilbo long before, and once a Hobbit – is by now on their trail, seeking back his lost Ring.

Boromir tries to seize the Ring by force to use against the enemy. A party of orcs attack, killing Boromir as he defends Frodo's Hobbit friends, Merry and Pippin. Frodo and his loyal companion Sam have, by now, parted from the rest of the company, heading east towards their destination, Mordor. The remainder of the Company follow the track of the orcs who have captured Merry and Pippin, going westwards.

The story now follows the progress of Frodo and Sam, and the others remaining in the Company, in parallel.

After the capture of Merry and Pippin by orcs, they are tracked by Aragorn, Legolas the Elf, and Gimli the Dwarf to the Forest of Fangorn, where the two Hobbits are hiding after escaping the orcs. In the Forest, the Hobbits meet Treebeard, guardian of the woodland. He is an Ent, a tree-creature. The Ents assault and capture Isengard, the stronghold of the traitor Saruman, a Wizard like Gandalf. Here the Hobbits are reunited with others of the Company, as well as Gandalf, returned from the dead.

Joining the forces of Théoden, the aged king of Rohan, most of the Company move towards the ancient city of Minas Tirith, now under threat from Sauron's forces. Aragorn, Legolas, and Gimli, however, pass through the Paths of the Dead to gather the spirits of long-dead warriors bound by a dreadful oath. These they lead southwards to attack the enemy there.

Meanwhile, Frodo and Sam move slowly towards Mordor, now led by the treacherous Gollum, intent on betrayal, yet held back by the vestiges of his lost nature. Finding the main entrance to Mordor impassable, Frodo accepts Gollum's offer to show them a secret entrance. There he leads them into the giant spider Shelob's Lair. After many perils (including the near death of Frodo) the two make their hopeless way to Mount Doom. At the final moment, Frodo cannot throw the Ring into the Cracks of Doom. Gollum bites off the ring finger, but falls to his death with the Ring. The quest is over. As Mordor disintegrates, and the wraith of Sauron fades, Frodo and Sam are rescued by eagles and reunited with their friends, where they are hailed as heroes.

Without the destruction of the Ring, the alliance against the dark powers of Mordor would have failed. Though there was no certainty of the success of the quest of Frodo and Sam, the people of Gondor and Rohan, and the other allies, were prepared to fight to the death against the dreadful enemy.

The story ends with the gradual healing of the land, preparing the way for the possession of humankind, now free from the threat of slavery. The fading of the Elves is complete as the last ships pass over the sea to the Undying Lands far off in the West. Joining the Elves are the Ring-bearers Bilbo and Frodo. Sam follows later, after a happy life in the Shire with his beloved Rosie.

The ordinary life of the Hobbits of the Shire was closer to Tolkien's own existence in the years up to the publication of *The Lord of the Rings* than the perilous quest to destroy the Ring, or fighting in the great battles of Helm's Deep or Pelennor Fields. Yet he felt that the writing of the book was his "war effort" in the continuing fight to establish good over evil. Thinking of the First World War, he believed that there could be no war to end all wars. As his friend C.S. Lewis remarked, "The war creates no absolutely new situation: it simply aggravates the permanent human situation so that we can no longer ignore it." But the purpose of all battle can only be to allow ordinary human life to continue and flourish. Any other purpose was to be supping with the devil.

So the years of the increasing popularity of *The Lord of the Rings,* and Tolkien's other fictional works, continued. Up to 2007, the estimated sales (treating multi-volume editions as one book) of *The Lord of the Rings* were 150 million. For comparison of increasing demand, we can look at the growth in print runs (in hardback, unless otherwise stated). The initial print run of *The Hobbit* in the UK (1937) was 1,500; the first printing in the UK of *The Fellowship of the Ring* was 3,000 (the US first printing that year was 1,500 copies); the first US paperback edition (1965) of *The Fellowship of the Ring*, which was unauthorized, was 150,000 copies; and the print run of the first edition in the UK of *The Silmarillion* was 375,000 copies. The US first printing of *The Silmarillion* (1977) was also 375,000 copies. The first US paperback edition of *The Silmarillion,* in 1979, had a print run of 2,515,000 before publication![8]

It was not long before Tolkien was to regret not taking early retirement; his royalty payments were eventually exceeding his pay packet from Oxford University. In the fifties most men did not live until retirement age, but were still working when they died. Hardly any were therefore able to enjoy even a few years of retirement. Tolkien was sixty-two when *The Lord of the Rings* appeared. He was to continue his duties as Merton Professor of English Language and Literature for another five years, even though the arthritis in his hands meant that he could barely write, and in May 1958 he fainted through stress, breaking his glasses and hurting his head. He rejected medical advice then to spend time in a nursing home, because of his need to look after Edith, just as, nearly twelve years before, in July 1946, he had ignored his doctor's prescription to rest for six months after getting close to another nervous breakdown.

In 1959, however, he retired, having run his course. He had not given the usual inaugural address when taking up the post, so he gave a valedictory one instead. He said, "Philology is the foundation of humane letters." Referring to his birth in South Africa, he observed: "I have the hatred of *apartheid* in my bones; and most of all I detest the segregation or separation of Language and Literature. I do not care which of them you think White."[9]

Throughout his period as Merton Professor of English Language and Literature, Tolkien had continued to explore and teach the language and literature of the West Midlands in the Middle English period. On 15 April 1953 he delivered the W.P. Ker Memorial Lecture at Glasgow University on *Sir Gawain and the Green Knight*. Later that year, in December, BBC radio broadcast a dramatization of Tolkien's translation of the same. Characteristically, he had drafted and redrafted the script of his introduction to the translation a number of times. His desire was to communicate the splendour of the poem both as a story and in its rich language and metre. In 1955 his poem "Imram" was published in *Time & Tide*. In "Imram" (Gaelic for "voyage") Tolkien adapted the legend of St Brendan's famous early medieval voyage to fit his invented mythology, while still celebrating its Celtic Christian vision. The poem alludes to the Lost Road, a "shoreless mountain" (Meneltarma) marking "the foundered land" (Númenor), a mysterious island (Tol Eressëa) with a white tree (Celeborn), and a beautiful star (Eärendil) marking the old road leading beyond the world. It indicated Tolkien's continuing desire to find a bridge for the contemporary reader to his mythology of "The Silmarillion".

One of Tolkien's achievements in this period was to persuade his friend C.S. Lewis to accept an invitation from Cambridge University to take on a new Chair that seemed tailored for him – Professor of Renaissance and Medieval Literature. Lewis had turned down the invitation not once, but twice. He feared leaving his brother Warren, who regularly went through intense struggles because of his alcoholism. As one of the Electors for the post, Tolkien knew exactly what was going on, and of course he knew his friend. He systematically allayed Lewis's fears over a number of issues, but, most importantly, the issue of Warren. He assured Lewis that the residency arrangements at Cambridge were flexible. In the end, Lewis arranged to commute to Cambridge some days each week during term time, living there in his rooms at Magdalene College. Even the weekly meetings of the Inklings in the Eagle and Child pub were moved from the hallowed Tuesdays to Monday mornings, to suit Lewis's travelling arrangements. While he was absent in Cambridge, Tolkien had gently pointed out, there was Fred Paxford (Lewis's handyman) and Len and Maude Miller (the housekeeper and her husband looking after Lewis's Headington home) to keep Warren company.

Retirement meant for Tolkien, among many things, the loss of his rooms at Merton College. The storage of his many books therefore became a problem, so he decided to convert his garage to a study-cum-office. Philip Norman, an interviewer from *The Sunday Times,* described the house some years afterwards, when the public had begun to be interested in Tolkien.[10] It was a three-bedroomed house that looked to the journalist just like a church rectory. It was near the Oxford United football ground, so football fans invaded the street outside whenever there were matches playing. "The study in the garage," the journalist wrote, "is filled with books and the smell of distinguished dust." Philip Norman also observed that the study contained a new tin clock and an ancient portmanteau, almost buried under some newspapers. Tolkien explained that the faded leather trunk had been given to him by his "half-Spaniard" guardian (that is, Father Francis Morgan). He had only kept it because inside were "all the things I've been going to answer for so many years, I've forgotten what they are". On the window ledge were tacked two papers. One was a map of Middle-earth that showed the routes of the two Hobbit quests – Bilbo's and Frodo's. The other was a list of Tolkien's engagements, in his bold handwriting.

There had been a glimpse into the future of how his fictional creations would eclipse his straight academic endeavours back in October 1954, a little over two months after the publication of *The Fellowship of the Ring*. He had travelled to the University of Liège in Belgium to receive an honorary Doctorate (Doct. en Lettres et Phil.). He was astonished to be welcomed in the ceremony as "le createur de M. Bilbo Baggins". After the resulting applause he was even more startled over the explanation that he was a "set book". There would be many more shocks of celebrity.

13

The Tolkien phenomenon, and farewell

The rest, as they say, is history. To fully describe the reception of Tolkien's work in the sixties and beyond would take another book. In many countries he is now a household name. One, New Zealand, has become an unofficial "Middle-earth" because of the Peter Jackson films. But meanwhile, through all the burgeoning excitement, Tolkien and Edith lived their ordinary lives through the decade of the sixties and to their deaths. That ordinary life is what they wanted to celebrate.

Before Tolkien's retirement Edith had been able to accompany her husband on one of his many trips to Ireland as an external examiner. They took annual holidays and after Priscilla left home, had been able to have their first one together for over twenty years, staying in the Lodge at Stonyhurst College, Lancashire. On a more epic scale, Edith had a Mediterranean cruise with friends, while Tolkien, accompanied by Priscilla, took a long train journey from Calais to Italy. On the way they passed near the Aletsch

Glacier that Tolkien had explored so very many years before. Eventually they arrived in Venice. In Italy Tolkien experienced the haunting feeling "of having come to the heart of Christendom" as an exile returning home "from the borders and far provinces".[1] After some days, they travelled by train to Assisi, visiting the tomb of St Francis, among other places. As the retirement years started to roll out, Edith and Tolkien enjoyed holidays in Bournemouth, staying at the Hotel Miramar. This was in a built-up area on the clifftops, so there were views over the sea, with glimpses of the Isle of Wight in the distance, and paths that made their way down the cliffs to the shore.

Sales of the three hardback volumes of *The Lord of the Rings* continued to bring in substantial sums, so that the Tolkiens were comfortably off. Fan mail began to pour in, soon beyond Tolkien's capacity to reply. This was before a strange quirk of US Copyright Law (since tightened up) helped to make *The Lord of the Rings* an international cultural phenomenon. Around late spring of 1965, Ace Books published an unauthorized paperback edition, exploiting a loophole in the law. A Tolkien fan society set up by Dick Plotz earlier that year began to support Tolkien's campaign against Ace Books. The word got around that fans should obtain an official edition by Ballantine Books rather than the one that did not pay any royalties to Tolkien for his work. The resulting publicity for Plotz's society helped it to grow enormously, and to bring Tolkien's name into the mainstream of American youth culture. Because of the international connections of an emerging counterculture in the US, throughout Europe, and elsewhere, the world of Hobbits, Wizards and the Shire helped to express a hippie culture. One of the most vibrant expressions was via rock music, with bands such as Led Zeppelin referring to Tolkien's stories in their compositions. The Beatles even planned to make a film of *The Lord of the Rings* with themselves in lead roles. Slogans like "Gandalf for President" and "Frodo Lives" were everywhere. One of the Inklings, Nevill Coghill, may have coined a phrase that became popular: "Tolkien is Hobbit-forming".[2] Certainly, during 1969 the slogan was spotted on a wall in Balliol College, Oxford.[3] In due course, the fan base and enormous readership of Tolkien throughout the globe made viable the production of Peter Jackson's lavish films of *The Lord of the Rings* and later *The Hobbit*.

Tolkien was not the kind of person to receive confidence and energy from celebrity. Indeed, this kind of attention was an irritant, intruding into the quiet life that he and Edith sought. One academic foolishly published Tolkien's home telephone number in a study of C.S. Lewis. However they obtained it, youthful American fans unaware of the time differences would sometimes ring Tolkien's telephone number in the early hours, disrupting sleep. In the end, Tolkien and Edith decided to move from Oxford to more congenial accommodation, and away from the attention of fans. Their choice was the coastal resort of Bournemouth, on the south coast, a favourite of the retired. Money was no difficulty, and they soon found a modest bungalow, 19 Lakeside Road, which meant no stairs for the increasingly arthritic Edith to climb. It was in a prosperous part of the town. Edith's experience was that it was easier to make friends in Bournemouth than in Oxford. They kept their address and other details secret from all but their family, Tolkien's publisher, and similar. Bournemouth is not far from

Milford-on-Sea, to which Tolkien's surviving friend from the T.C.B.S., Christopher Wiseman, had retired, and they had some contact.

The celebrity years, in fact, marked something of a crisis in Tolkien's life, on top of the inevitable decline in his health and that of Edith, who was three years older. He had described the death of C.S. Lewis in November 1963 as like an axe blow near his very roots. (To think of himself as a tree was characteristic of Tolkien.) Perhaps he took some consolation from something that Lewis had written to him the Christmas before his death: "All my philosophy of history hangs upon a sentence of your own, 'Deeds were done which were not *wholly* in vain.'" The sentence is from *The Fellowship of the Ring*, which had been read to Lewis long ago: "There was sorrow then too, and gathering dark, but great valour, and great deeds that were not wholly vain." His friend had clearly drawn comfort from his words near the end of his life.

It was around this time that Tolkien wrote his last story published during his lifetime, *Smith of Wootton Major* (1967). This short story has some parallels with his famous essay "On Fairy Stories" in tracing the relationship between the world of faerie and the primary world we experience. The story seems deceptively simple at first. Tolkien described it as "an old man's book, already weighted with the presage of 'bereavement'". It was as if, like Smith in the story with his Elven star, Tolkien fully expected his imagination to fade away; it was a time of self-doubt for him. In a review, Roger Lancelyn Green wrote of the small book: "To seek for the meaning is to cut open the ball in search of its bounce." Like *Farmer Giles of Ham*, the story has an undefined medieval setting. The villages of Wootton Major and Minor could have come straight out of the Hobbits' Shire or, indeed, old Oxfordshire. As in Middle-earth, it is possible to walk in and out of the world of faerie (the realm of Elves). The story contains Alf, an Elven-king in disguise, apprentice to the bungling cake-maker Nokes. Nokes has no concept of the reality of faerie, but his sugary cake for the village children, adorned with its crude Fairy Queen doll, can stir the imagination of the humble. A magic Elven star found by Nokes and put in the cake is swallowed by Smith, then a child, giving him access to the fairy world. In the village it is the children who can be susceptible to the "other", the numinous, whereas their elders are only concerned with eating and drinking. The star eventually reappears and becomes attached to Smith's brow. Smith grows up to be a Master Smith ("he could work iron into wonderful forms that looked as light and delicate as a spray of leaves and blossom, but kept the stern strength of iron") and, in so far as the book has autobiographical elements, may be said to represent Tolkien himself, and his ability to spin tales of Elves and faerie.

As in Tolkien's earlier story *Leaf by Niggle,* glimpses of other worlds transform art and craft in human life, giving them an Elven or spiritual quality. The ordinary work of the village smith is seen in a new light, transformed into a new dimension, just as the humble work of the storyteller can suggest a reality beyond the "walls of the world".

During this period of self-doubt, which perhaps began soon after Lewis's death, the popularity of *The Lord of the Rings* exploded, though Tolkien only heard about the phenomenon gradually. One result was that he was forced to use a part-time secretary, who worked in the converted garage at Sandfield Road before the move to Bournemouth. In 1966 he and Edith celebrated their golden wedding anniversary. The occasion was marked by Donald Swann's performance of a cycle of songs, based upon poems from *The Hobbit* and *The Lord of the Rings*.

Tolkien eventually passed through this long shadow of doubt about his work, especially the unfinished "The Silmarillion", in which he had invested his life. He now believed that his work would not be "wholly vain". He continued to work on the cycle of legends in the final years of his life.

Edith was approaching eighty and Tolkien was seventy-six by 1968. Her severe arthritis made tending the house difficult, so the move to Bournemouth that year brought some relief. Tolkien pottered with diverse manuscripts of "The Silmarillion", bewildering in their variety, less troubled by interruptions. By 1971, he and Edith had settled into a comfortable routine that might eventually have led to a more consistent arrangement of the annals and tales of the earlier Ages of Middle-earth. However, Edith's health suddenly failed. She was hospitalized with an inflamed gall bladder and died a few days later, on 29 November 1971.

With the loss of Edith, his Lúthien, Tolkien had no reason to stay in Bournemouth. His old college, Merton, offered him an honorary fellowship and some rooms in a house belonging to the college. In March 1972, he gratefully moved into 21 Merton Street, near the college. In the last brief part of his life he was able to travel to see friends and family, take vacations, and visit Buckingham Palace to receive his CBE from the Queen. While on a visit to Bournemouth to stay with friends he was taken ill with an acute bleeding gastric ulcer, which led to a chest infection. Four days later, on Sunday, 2 September 1973, he died.

On their joint grave in Wolvercote Cemetery, in north Oxford, is inscribed, with reference to his tale of Beren and Lúthien from *The Silmarillion*:

+

EDITH MARY TOLKIEN

LUTHIEN

1889–1971

JOHN RONALD

REUEL TOLKIEN

BEREN

1892–1973

Afterword

By an almost superhuman effort, Tolkien's son Christopher edited an edition of his father's unfinished writings, published as *The Silmarillion* in 1977. More than anyone else, he understood his father's intentions. Though the book is compressed, and lacks an overall narrative framework (Tolkien failed to complete any of his options for this), it masterfully made available for readers the stories and annals of the Ages of Middle-earth before the period of *The Lord of the Rings*. It is presented as a coherent compendium of legends, stories, annals, and other elements. Subsequently, Christopher Tolkien has edited an enormous amount and variety of further material, for which the published *The Silmarillion* provides an overall picture. These are *Unfinished Tales,* and twelve volumes making up *The History of Middle-earth*. He has also edited various translations and retellings by Tolkien from Middle English and Old Norse.

Notes

1. "I am in fact a Hobbit…"

1. Through J.R.R. Tolkien's childhood and youth to his coming-of-age, I simply call him "Ronald", and "Tolkien" thereafter. He was called a variety of names at different times by various people – John, John Ronald, Tolkien, or even Tollers.

2. BBC Radio interview with Denys Gueroult, *Now Read On,* 16 December 1970.

3. *Ibid*.

4. Tolkien interviewed by John Ezard; quoted by Ezard in *The Guardian,* 28 December 1991.

5. Quoted by Humphrey Carpenter, *J.R.R. Tolkien: A Biography* (London: Unwin Paperbacks, 1978), p. 36.

6. Now called "Fern Cottage".

7. Quoted by Carpenter, *J.R.R. Tolkien: A Biography*, p. 37.

2. Edith

1. J.R.R. Tolkien (Humphrey Carpenter, ed.), *The Letters of J.R.R. Tolkien* (London: HarperCollins, 2006), p. 395.

2. Quoted by Mr Gerard Tracey on http://www.birmingham-oratory.org.uk/TheOratory/Tolkien/tabid/76/Default.aspx

3. Peter Jackson's *The Two Towers* comes down on the side of the towers being Orthanc and Barad-dûr, a possibility considered by Tolkien. In the story itself, there is no clear indication of this.

4. The Waterworks at Edgbaston: See Robert S. Blackham, *The Roots of Tolkien's Middle-earth* (Stroud: Tempus, 2006), p. 99.

5. *Ibid.*, p. 105.

6. http://domesdaymap.co.uk/place/SP0584/edgbaston/

7. See Blackham, *The Roots of Tolkien's Middle-earth*, p. 98 and http://en.wikipedia.org/wiki/Sampson_Gamgee

8. Blackham, *The Roots of Tolkien's Middle-earth*, p. 105.

9. Tolkien (Carpenter, ed.), *The Letters of J.R.R. Tolkien*, p. 416.

10. Richard Plotz, interview with Tolkien, "J.R.R. Tolkien Talks about the Discovery of Middle-earth, the Origins of Elvish", *Seventeen* (January 1967), p. 118.

11. *The Times* obituary of J.R.R. Tolkien, 3 September 1973.

12. The hotel no longer exists, and the building is in a poor state of repair. See: www.savethe3cups.info

13. The Index of Wills and Administration for 1891 contains the following entry for Alfred Frederick Warrillow (Personal Estate £8,724 15s. 2d.): "23 April. The Will of Alfred Frederick Warrillow late of Hudson House Strechford in the Parish of Yardley in the County of Worcester and of 101 Great-Hampton-street in the City of Birmingham Paper Dealer who died 12 March 1891 at Hudson House was proved at Worcester by Frances Bratt of Hudson House Spinster the sole Executrix."

3. Schooldays and the T.C.B.S.

1. Humphrey Carpenter, *J.R.R. Tolkien: A Biography* (London: Unwin Paperbacks, 1978), p. 53.

2. See John Garth, "Wiseman, Christopher", in Michael D.C. Drout (ed.), *J.R.R. Tolkien Encyclopedia* (New York and London: Routledge, 2007), pp. 708–709.

3. Carpenter, *J.R.R. Tolkien: A Biography*, p. 41.

4. *Ibid.*, pp. 53–54.

5. A. Douglas, D. Moore, and J. Douglas, *Birmingham Remembered: A Centenary Celebration* (Birmingham: The Birmingham Post & Mail, 1988), p. 103.

6. "The Musical and Dramatic Society", in *King Edward's School Chronicle*, n.s. 27, no. 191 (March 1912), p. 10 – quoted in Wayne G. Hammond and Christina Scull, *The J.R.R. Tolkien Companion and Guide: Chronology* (London: HarperCollins, 2006), pp. 30–31.

7. Carpenter, *J.R.R. Tolkien: A Biography,* p. 57.

8. Tom Shippey, *J.R.R. Tolkien: Author of the Century* (London: HarperCollins, 2001), p. xii.

9. J.R.R. Tolkien (Humphrey Carpenter, ed.), *The Letters of J.R.R. Tolkien* (London: HarperCollins, 2006), p. 357, 20 July 1965.

10. *Ibid.*, p. 213.

11. "English and Welsh", in J.R.R. Tolkien, *The Monsters and the Critics and Other Essays* (London: George Allen and Unwin, 1983), p. 191.

12. On G.B. Smith and other members of the T.C.B.S., see John Garth's definitive *Tolkien and the Great War* (London: HarperCollins, 2005).

13. Hammond and Scull, *The J.R.R. Tolkien Companion and Guide: Chronology*, p. 1045.

14. *King Edward's School Chronicle*, n.s. 27, no. 191 (March 1912), p. 4.

15. Quoted in Carpenter, *J.R.R. Tolkien: A Biography*, p. 55.

16. *Ibid.*, p. 58.

17. Tolkien (Carpenter, ed.), *The Letters of J.R.R. Tolkien*, no. 306.

18. *Ibid.*

19. Tolkien says as much, *The Letters of J.R.R. Tolkien*, p. 309.

20. C.S. Lewis, *An Experiment in Criticism* (Cambridge: Cambridge University Press, 1961), pp. 140–41.

4. Oxford and the dawn of a new life

1. After the First World War, his future friend C.S. Lewis would start his studies in the same school of Literae Humaniores. Lewis was six years Tolkien's junior.

2. These authors can be enjoyed in contemporary translation in the Penguin Classics series. Tolkien may have become, or already been, aware of Plato's creation account, *Timaeus,* at this time. It provides useful background reading for Tolkien's beautiful depiction of the creation of the universe and Middle-earth in the first section of "The Silmarillion" – his body of tales about, and accounts of, the early Ages of Middle-earth that forms the rich background of *The Hobbit* and *The Lord of the Rings.*

3. *The Times* obituary of J.R.R. Tolkien, 3 September 1973.

4. *Ibid.*

5. *Ibid.*

6. Wayne G. Hammond and Christina Scull, *The J.R.R. Tolkien Companion and Guide: Chronology* (London: HarperCollins, 2006), p. 34, quoting an "Oxford letter" by Oxoniensis to the *King Edward's School Chronicle,* Dec 1912.

7. Examples can be found in Wayne G. Hammond and Christina Scull, *J.R.R. Tolkien: Artist & Illustrator* (London: HarperCollins, 1995).

8. Humphrey Carpenter, *J.R.R. Tolkien: A Biography* (London: Unwin Paperbacks, 1978), p. 71.

9. Bodleian Library, Tolkien Special Collection, A21/1.

10. Wayne G. Hammond and Christina Scull, *The J.R.R. Tolkien Companion and Guide: Reader's Guide* (London: HarperCollins, 2006), p. 999.

11. The historic West Midlands region includes the counties of Herefordshire, Shropshire, Staffordshire, Worcestershire and Warwickshire, as well as the more recent West Midlands conurbation or metropolitan county, formed in 1974.

12. Not Victoria Road, as stated in Scull and Hammond, *The Tolkien Family Album,* and elsewhere.

5. *The shadow of war*

1. From time to time the Bodleian Library in Oxford displays some of his drawings and paintings, from its large archives.

2. John Garth, *Tolkien and the Great War* (London: HarperCollins, 2005), p. 8.

3. *Ibid.*, p. 9.

4. Martin Gilbert, *Somme: The Heroism and Horror of War* (London: John Murray, 2006), pp. 140–41; Garth, *Tolkien and the Great War*, p. 183.

5. Quoted by Humphrey Carpenter, *J. R. R. Tolkien: A Biography* (London: Unwin Paperbacks, 1978), p. 72.

6. From George Steiner, originally published in *Le Monde*, 6 September 1973, translated as "Tolkien, Oxford's Eccentric Don", in Douglas A. Anderson, Michael D.C. Drout, and Verlyn Flieger (eds), *Tolkien Studies*: Volume 5 (West Virginia University Press, 2008), pp. 186–88.

7. For more on this, see Dimitra Fimi's lucid account, *Tolkien, Race and Cultural History* (Basingstoke: Palgrave Macmillan, 2010), p. 9.

8. Carpenter, *J. R. R. Tolkien: A Biography*, p. 79.

9. Fimi, *Tolkien, Race and Cultural History*, p. 16.

10. Carpenter, *J. R. R. Tolkien: A Biography*, p. 80.

11. J.R.R. Tolkien (Humphrey Carpenter, ed.), *The Letters of J. R. R. Tolkien* (London: HarperCollins, 2006), Letter 105 (letter to Christopher Tolkien).

12. See Wayne G. Hammond and Christina Scull, *The J. R. R. Tolkien Companion and Guide: Chronology* (London: HarperCollins, 2006), p. 56.

13. Garth, *Tolkien and the Great War*, pp. 58, 60.

14. John Garth, "T.C.B.S. (Tea Club and Barrovian Society)", in Michael D.C. Drout (ed.), *J. R. R. Tolkien Encyclopedia* (New York and London: Routledge, 2007), p. 635.

6. *War and loss*

1. Quoted by John Garth, *Tolkien and the Great War* (London: HarperCollins, 2005), p. 101, from a letter to Tolkien, 6 October 1915.

2. In Thiepval Wood on the Somme (the scene of some of the fiercest fighting in the Battle of the Somme later that year), according to Garth, *Tolkien and the Great War*, p. 117

3. *Ibid.*, p. 117.

4. *Ibid.*, pp. 118–119.

5. See Robert S. Blackham, *Tolkien and the Peril of War* (Stroud: The History Press, 2011), p. 63.

6. There is a lively debate about the location of a source "the House of a Hundred Chimneys", with alternative suggestions put forward. See Blackham, *Tolkien and the Peril of War*, p. 63; also Wayne G. Hammond and Christina Scull, *The J.R.R. Tolkien Companion and Guide: Reader's Guide* (London: HarperCollins, 2006), pp. 351–52.

7. Bill Cater, "We talked of love, death and fairy tales", *The Daily Telegraph,* 29 November, 2001, p. 23. http://www.telegraph.co.uk/culture/4726863/We-talked-of-love-death-and-fairy-tales.html.

8. For more on Lanky, see http://www.paulsalveson.org.uk/northern-voices-dialect-writing-of-lancashire-and-yorkshire/

9. Quoted in Humphrey Carpenter, *J.R.R. Tolkien: A Biography* (London: Unwin Paperbacks, 1978), p. 89.

10. Letter to Tolkien, 22 June 1916, quoted by Garth, *Tolkien and the Great War,* p. 146.

11. The Celtic word might be *samara,* "tranquil"; see John Everett-Heath, *Concise Dictionary of World Place-Names* (Oxford: Oxford University Press, 2005).

12. Quoted by Martin Gilbert, *Somme: The Heroism and Horror of War* (London: John Murray, 2006), pp. xvii, 37, 44, 208.

13. *Ibid.,* p. xvii.

14. See http://history-world.org/world_war_one.htm

15. Quoted in Gilbert, *Somme: The Heroism and Horror of War,* p. 140–41.

16. For Tolkien's initial response to the death of Gilson: see J.R.R. Tolkien (Humphrey Carpenter, ed.), *The Letters of J.R.R. Tolkien* (London: HarperCollins, 2006), Letter 5, from Tolkien to Smith, 12 August 1916.

17. Quoted in Gilbert, *Somme: The Heroism and Horror of War,* p. 201.

18. Philip Norman, "The Hobbit Man", *Sunday Times Magazine,* 15 January 1967.

7. Recovery, "W", and half a million words

1. Quoted in Judith Priestman, *Tolkien: Life and Legend* (Oxford: Bodleian Library, 1992), p. 34.

2. BBC Radio interview with Denys Gueroult, *Now Read On,* 16 December 1970.

3. I am indebted to John Garth for this insight. See John Garth, *Tolkien and the Great War* (London: HarperCollins, 2005), pp. 220–21.

4. Reported in *The Times,* 25 October 1916, from the German source, the *Düsseldorfer Generalanzeiger,* as cited in John Garth, *Tolkien and the Great War*, p. 221.

5. Larry D. Benson (ed.), *The Riverside Chaucer* (Oxford: OUP, 2008), p. 129.

6. Garth, *Tolkien and the Great War*, p. 238; Robert S. Blackham, *Tolkien and the Peril of War* (Stroud: The History Press, 2011), pp. 143–44.

7. J.R.R. Tolkien (Humphrey Carpenter, ed.), *The Letters of J.R.R. Tolkien* (London: HarperCollins, 2006), Letter 340, p. 420.

8. See Wayne G. Hammond and Christina Scull, *J.R.R. Tolkien: Artist & Illustrator* (London: HarperCollins, 1995), pp. 26, 31.

9. Quoted in Humphrey Carpenter, *J.R.R. Tolkien: A Biography* (London: Unwin Paperbacks, 1978), p. 106.

10. Peter Gilliver, Jeremy Marshall, and Edmund Weiner, *The Ring of Words: Tolkien and the Oxford English Dictionary* (Oxford: Oxford University Press, 2006), p. vii.

11. *Ibid.*

12. *Ibid.*, p. viii.

13. *Ibid.*

14. Tolkien (Carpenter, ed.), *The Letters of J.R.R. Tolkien*, Letter 89, p. 100.

15. Exeter College archives, quoted in Wayne G. Hammond and Christina Scull, *The J.R.R. Tolkien Companion and Guide: Chronology* (London: HarperCollins, 2006), p. 111; spelling corrections mine).

8. Leeds and dragons

1. C.S. Lewis, *Selected Literary Essays* (CUP, 1969), p. 18. Format simplified.

2. See Wayne G. Hammond and Christina Scull, *The J.R.R. Tolkien Companion and Guide: Reader's Guide* (London: HarperCollins, 2006), pp. 858–60.

3. Humphrey Carpenter, *J.R.R. Tolkien: A Biography* (London: Unwin Paperbacks, 1978), p. 113.

4. Letter to Ken Jackson, 29 January 1968, quoted in http://www.tolkienlibrary.com/collecting/seenonebay/object17/description.htm.

5. See Carpenter, *J.R.R. Tolkien: A Biography,* p. 114.

6. Quoted in Carpenter, *J.R.R. Tolkien: A Biography*, p. 138.

7. T.A. Shippey, "Tolkien, John Ronald Reuel (1892–1973)", in *Oxford Dictionary of National Biography* (Oxford University Press, 2004); online edn., Oct 2006.

9. Oxford and C.S. Lewis

1. J.I.M. Stewart, *A Memorial Service* (London: Magnum Books, Methuen Paperbacks Ltd, 1977), p. 176.

2. W.H. Auden, "Making, Knowing and Judging", in W.H. Auden, *The Dyer's Hand and Other Essays* (New York: Random House, 1962), pp. 41–42.

3. Quoted in Humphrey Carpenter, *J.R.R. Tolkien: A Biography* (London: Unwin Paperbacks, 1978), p. 138.

4. John Lucas, "Auden's politics: power, authority and the individual", in Stan Smith (ed.), *The Cambridge Companion to W.H. Auden* (Cambridge: Cambridge University Press, 2004), p. 152.

5. Edward Mendelson, "The European Auden", in Smith (ed.), *The Cambridge Companion to W.H. Auden* , p. 62.

6. Quoted in William Ready, *The Tolkien Relation* (Chicago: Regnery, 1968), p. 17.

7. Quoted in Zachary Leader, *The Life of Kingsley Amis* (London: Jonathan Cape, 2006), p. 123.

8. *Ibid.*

9. Kingsley Amis, *Memoirs* (London: Penguin Books, 1992), p. 45.

10. Carpenter, *J.R.R. Tolkien: A Biography,* p. 158.

11. *Ibid.*, p. 159.

12. J.I.M. Stewart, *Young Pattullo* (London: Gollancz, 1975), pp. 106–108.

13. John and Priscilla Tolkien, *The Tolkien Family Album* (London: Unwin.Hyman, 1992), p. 50.

14. Diary of C.S. Lewis, Tuesday 11 May, 1926. See Walter Hooper (ed.), *All My Road Before Me: The Diary of C.S. Lewis 1922–27* (London: HarperCollins, 1991).

15. *The Times* obituary of J.R.R. Tolkien, 3 September 1973.

16. John Mabbott, *Oxford Memories* (Oxford: Thornton's of Oxford, 1986), p. 73.

17. In *Oxford Magazine,* 48, No. 21, 1930.

18. Quoted in Humphrey Carpenter, *The Inklings: C. S. Lewis, J. R. R. Tolkien, Charles Williams, and their friends* (Boston: Houghton Mifflin, 1979), p. 42.

19. From Houghton Mifflin webpages, http://www.hmhbooks.com/features/lordoftheringstrilogy/bio.jsp

20. A.N. Wilson, *C.S. Lewis: A Biography* (London: Collins, 1990), p. 117.

21. Letter to Tolkien, 7 December 1929, quoted in J.R.R. Tolkien, *The Lays of Beleriand*, p. 151.

22. Helen Gardner, "Clive Staples Lewis (1898–1963)", *Proc. British Academy 51* (1965), pp. 417–28.

23. C.S. Lewis, *Surprised by Joy* in C.S. Lewis, *Selected Books* (London: Harper Collins, 1999), p. 1369.

10. Of Hobbits and Inklings

1. Published after his death in J.R.R. Tolkien, *Unfinished Tales of Númenor and Middle-earth* (London: George Allen and Unwin, 1980).

2. For more on this, see John D. Rateliff, *The History of the Hobbit*, 2 volumes (HarperCollins, 2007).

3. In J.R.R. Tolkien, *The Hobbit*, 1987 ed. (London: Unwin Hyman), p. vii.

4. Quoted by Humphrey Carpenter, *J.R.R. Tolkien: A Biography* (London: Unwin Paperbacks, 1978), p. 184.

5. *New York Times*, October 31, 1954.

6. "On Fairy Stories", in J.R.R. Tolkien, *The Monsters and the Critics and Other Essays* (London: George Allen and Unwin, 1983), p. 151.

7. John Lawlor, *Memories and Reflections* (Dallas: Spence Publishing Company, 1998), pp. 33–35.

8. Quoted in Carpenter, *J.R.R. Tolkien: A Biography*, p. 152.

9. See Tolkien's undated letter to Anne Barrett in 1956, in J.R.R.

Tolkien (Humphrey Carpenter, ed.), *The Letters of J.R.R. Tolkien* (London: HarperCollins, 2006), p. 238.

10. Donald K. Fry, *The Beowulf poet: a collection of critical essays* (Englewood Cliffs, New Jersey: Prentice-Hall, 1968), p. ix.

11. Tolkien's second war

1. It is possible that Tolkien's duties as an air-raid warden had begun soon after the London Blitz (heavy bombing), which started in September 1940.

2. John and Priscilla Tolkien, *The Tolkien Family Album* (London: Unwin/Hyman), p. 55.

3. C.S. Lewis, *Arthurian Torso: Containing the Posthumous Fragment of "The Figure of Arthur" by Charles Williams and a Commentary on the Arthurian Poems of Charles Williams by C.S. Lewis* (London: Oxford University Press, 1948), p. 2.

4. T.S. Eliot, "Introduction", in Charles Williams, *All Hallows' Eve* (New York: The Noonday Press, 1977), pp. xiii–xxiv, xviii.

5. See Humphrey Carpenter, *J.R.R. Tolkien: A Biography* (London: Unwin Paperbacks, 1978), p. 199.

6. J.R.R. Tolkien (Humphrey Carpenter, ed.), *The Letters of J.R.R. Tolkien* (London: HarperCollins, 2006), Letter 96, p. 111.

7. *Ibid.*, Letter 66, p. 78.

12. The struggle to publish

1. J.R.R. Tolkien, Foreword to *The Fellowship of the Ring* (London: George Allen and Unwin, 1954), p. 7.

2. See the BBC television coverage of the occasion at http://www.bbc.co.uk/archive/princesselizabeth/6621.shtml

3. J.R.R. Tolkien (Humphrey Carpenter, ed.), *The Letters of J.R.R. Tolkien* (London: HarperCollins, 2006), Letter 142, p. 172.

4. BBC Radio interview with Denys Gueroult, *Now Read On,* 16 December 1970.

5. Tolkien (Carpenter, ed.), *The Letters of J.R.R. Tolkien*, p. 122.

6. George Sayer, "Recollections of J.R.R. Tolkien", in Patricia Reynolds and Glen H. GoodKnight (eds), *Proceedings of the J.R.R. Tolkien Centenary Conference 1992* (Milton Keynes: Tolkien Society; Altadena, California: Mythopoeic Press, 1995), p. 23.

7. Clyde S. Kilby and Marjorie Lamp Mead (eds), *Brothers and Friends: The Diaries of Major Warren Hamilton Lewis* (New York: Ballantine Books, 1988), pp. 233–34. There's no Pring Rd in Malvern; it may be a transcription error for "Spring Lane".

8. Statistics from Wayne G. Hammond, *J.R.R. Tolkien: A Descriptive Bibliography* (Winchester: St Paul's Bibliographies and New Castle, Delaware: Oak Knoll Books, 1993).

9. "Valedictory Address", in J.R.R. Tolkien, *The Monsters and the Critics and Other Essays* (London: George Allen and Unwin, 1983), p. 238.

10. Philip Norman, "The Hobbit Man", *Sunday Times Magazine*, 15 January 1967.

13. The Tolkien phenomenon, and farewell

1. Wayne G. Hammond and Christina Scull, *The J.R.R. Tolkien Companion and Guide: Chronology* (London: HarperCollins, 2006), p. 464.

2. Tolkien attributes the adjective "Hobbit-forming" to him in a letter to Roger Lancelyn Green, 8 January 1971, in J.R.R. Tolkien (Humphrey Carpenter, ed.), *The Letters of J.R.R. Tolkien* (London: HarperCollins, 2006), Letter 319, pp. 406–407.

3. *The Bookseller,* 1968 series, p. 2136.

Select bibliography

Amis, Kingsley, *Memoirs* (London: Penguin Books, 1992).

Anderson, Douglas A., Michael D.C. Drout, and Verlyn Flieger (eds), *Tolkien Studies*: Volume 5 (West Virginia University Press, 2008).

Blackham, Robert S., *The Roots of Tolkien's Middle-earth* (Stroud: Tempus, 2006).

Blackham, Robert S., *Tolkien's Oxford* (Stroud: The History Press, 2008).

Blackham, Robert S., *Tolkien and the Peril of War* (Stroud: The History Press, 2011).

Carpenter, Humphrey, *J.R.R. Tolkien: A Biography* (London: Unwin Paperbacks, 1978).

Carpenter, Humphrey, *The Inklings: C. S. Lewis, J. R. R. Tolkien, Charles Williams, and their friends* (Boston: Houghton Mifflin, 1979), p. 42.

Carpenter, Humphrey (ed.), *The Letters of J.R.R. Tolkien* (London: HarperCollins, 2006).

Cater, Bill, "We talked of love, death and fairy tales", *The Daily Telegraph,* 29 November 2001.

Douglas, A., D. Moore and J. Douglas, *Birmingham Remembered: A Centenary Celebration* (Birmingham: The Birmingham Post & Mail, 1988).

Drout, Michael D.C. (ed.), *J.R.R. Tolkien Encyclopedia* (New York and London: Routledge, 2007).

Duriez, Colin, *J.R.R. Tolkien and C.S. Lewis: The Story of Their Friendship* (Stroud: Sutton Publishing, 2003).

Duriez, Colin, *Tolkien and The Lord of the Rings: A Guide to Middle-earth* (Stroud: The History Press, 2004).

Fimi, Dimitra, *Tolkien, Race and Cultural History* (Basingstoke: Palgrave Macmillan, 2010).

Garth, John, *Tolkien and the Great War* (London: HarperCollins, 2005).

Gilbert, Martin, *Somme: The Heroism and Horror of War* (London: John Murray, 2006).

Gilbert, Martin, "What Tolkien Taught Me about the Battle of the Somme", *The Cutting Edge,* August 5, 2008.

Gilliver, Peter, Jeremy Marshall, and Edmund Weiner, *The Ring of Words: Tolkien and the Oxford English Dictionary* (Oxford: Oxford University Press, 2006).

Gueroult, Denys, *Now Read On,* BBC Radio interview with J.R.R. Tolkien, 16 December 1970.

Hammond, Wayne G., *J.R.R. Tolkien: A Descriptive Bibliography* (Winchester: St Paul's Bibliographies and New Castle, Delaware: Oak Knoll Books, 1993).

Hammond, Wayne G. and Christina Scull, *J.R.R. Tolkien: Artist & Illustrator* (London: HarperCollins, 1995).

Hooper, Walter (ed.), *All My Road Before Me: The Diary of C.S. Lewis 1922–27* (London: HarperCollins, 1991).

Kilby, Clyde S., *Tolkien and the Silmarillion* (Wheaton, Ill.: Harold Shaw, 1976).

Kilby, Clyde S. and Marjorie Lamp Mead (eds), *Brothers and Friends: The Diaries of Major Warren Hamilton Lewis* (New York: Ballantine Books, 1988).

Lawlor, John, *Memories and Reflections* (Dallas: Spence Publishing Company, 1998).

Leader, Zachary, *The Life of Kingsley Amis* (London: Jonathan Cape, 2006).

Lewis, C.S., *An Experiment in Criticism* (Cambridge: Cambridge University Press, 1961).

Lewis, C.S., *Selected Literary Essays* (CUP, 1969).

Norman, Philip, "The Hobbit Man", *Sunday Times Magazine*, 15 January 1967.

Priestman, Judith, *Tolkien: Life and Legend* (Oxford: Bodleian Library, 1992).

Rateliff, John D., *The History of the Hobbit*, 2 volumes (HarperCollins, 2007).

Ready, William, *The Tolkien Relation* (Chicago: Regnery, 1968).

Reynolds, Patricia, and Glen H. GoodKnight (eds), *Proceedings of the J.R.R. Tolkien Centenary Conference 1992* (Milton Keynes: Tolkien Society; Altadena, California: Mythopoeic Press, 1995).

Scull, Christina, and Wayne G. Hammond, *The J.R.R. Tolkien Companion and Guide: Chronology* (London: HarperCollins, 2006).

Scull, Christina, and Wayne G. Hammond, *The J.R.R. Tolkien Companion and Guide: Reader's Guide* (London: HarperCollins, 2006).

Shippey, Tom, *J.R.R. Tolkien: Author of the Century* (London: HarperCollins, 2001).

Shippey, T.A., "Tolkien, John Ronald Reuel (1892–1973)", in *Oxford Dictionary of National Biography* (Oxford University Press, 2004); online edn, Oct 2006.

Smith, Stan (ed.), *The Cambridge Companion to W. H. Auden* (Cambridge: Cambridge University Press, 2004).

Stewart, J.I.M., *Young Pattullo* (London: Gollancz, 1975).

The Times obituary of J.R.R. Tolkien, 3 September 1973.

Tolkien, J.R.R., *Unfinished Tales of Númenor and Middle-earth* (London: George Allen and Unwin, 1980).

Tolkien, J.R.R., *The Monsters and the Critics and Other Essays* (London: George Allen and Unwin, 1983).

Tolkien, John and Priscilla, *The Tolkien Family Album* (London: Unwin/Hyman, 1992).

Wilson, A.N., *C.S. Lewis: A Biography* (London: Collins, 1990).

Index

Aletsch Glacier 51, 52, 213

Amis, Kingsley 135–36

Aristophanes 50

Auden, W.H. 46, 133–35, 146, 158, 204

Austen, Jane 31

Austin, Olney 148

"Bag End" Farm 129

Barfield, Owen 146–47, 169–170

Barnsley, T.K. "Tea-Cake" 47, 61, 84, 104

Barnt Green, Worcestershire 29, 55

Barrovian Society 42

Barrowclough, Sydney 47–48, 61, 84

Barry, Sir Charles 17

BBC 13, 18, 182, 199, 210

The Beatles 215

Beowulf 73, 110, 124, 134–35, 147–48, 173–75

Birmingham and vicinity 15, 17–19, 28, 93, 101, 133
  Ashfield Road, King's Heath 14
  Barrow's Stores 42, 44
  Birmingham University 101
  Corporation Street 42, 44
  Edgbaston, *see separate entry*
  Five Ways 26
  Handsworth 33
  Hurst Green 51
  King Edward's School 17, 19, 26, 33, 35, 38–41, 43–50, 58–61, 76, 114, 134
  King's Heath 14, 18
  King's Norton 25
  Lickey Hills 21, 31, 35
  Moseley 17, 18, 29
  New Street 17, 26, 93, 101
  Rednal 21, 29, 35
  Sarehole 15–17, 21, 23, 59, 129
  Sarehole Mill 15–17
  Selly Oak 101
  Strechford 222
  Woodside Cottage 20–21, 24, 35

Blackham, Robert 9, 28

Blackpool 114

Bletchley Park, Bedfordshire 178

Bloemfontein, South Africa 11–12, 14

Bournemouth 71, 214–18,

Bradley, Henry 117

Bratt, Frances 33–34, 67, 69, 112, 222

Brewerton, George 49–50

Brocton Camp, Staffordshire 90

Bromsgrove, Worcestershire 21

Cambridge 47–48, 57, 61, 142, 144, 210–11

Cannock Chase 90–91, 93, 113

Cape Town 7, 12, 13

Carpenter, Humphrey 9, 30, 33, 38, 41–42, 50, 56, 66, 69, 75, 97, 128, 134, 138, 140, 165

Cecil, Lord David 194

Chaucer, Geoffrey 49–50, 66–67, 108

Cheltenham 36, 62–63, 68, 112, 139

Clevedon, Somerset 87

The Coalbiters 151–52, 171
Coghill, Nevill 119, 151–52, 194, 215
Council of Lichfield 88
Council of London 82–83
Craigie, William, 115
Cullis, Colin 80, 116–17
Dagnell, Susan 158
Darnley Road, Leeds 129, 131, 138
Dents Garth, Roos 109
Dinard, France 71
Dormston, Worcestershire 129
Dresden House School, Evesham 34, 196
Drogo of Edgbaston 28
Dyson, H.V.D. "Hugo" 119, 167–68, 182–83, 189, 192, 194
Edgbaston 18–19, 24–28, 93
    Duchess Road 32, 34
    Highfield Road 36
    The Ivy Bush 29
    Oliver Road 19
    Birmingham Oratory 18–21, 24–27, 29, 32, 35, 43, 68, 87
    Perrott's Folly 27
    Plough and Harrow Hotel 93
    Rotton Park Reservoir 28
    St Philip's School 19–20, 41
    Stirling Road 25, 27, 29, 32
    the "two towers" 27–28, 221
    Waterworks Road 27
    Waterworks Tower 28
Eliot, T.S. 185
Étaples, France 93
Evesham 23, 34, 57, 128, 162, 164, 196
Ezard, John 221
Faulkner, Mrs 32, 34
Field, George 37, 62–63
Filey, Yorkshire 125–26, 128
Fimi, Dimitra 9, 79
Flamborough Head, Yorkshire 128

Fowles, John 32
Fry, Donald K. 173
Gamgee, Dr Joseph Sampson 29
Gardner 153
Garth, John 9, 56, 83, 222, 223
Gateley, Stephen 34, 64
George Hotel, Lichfield 88
Gilson, Robert Quilter 43–44, 47, 61, 76, 82–84, 88, 90, 94–98
Gipsy Green, Staffordshire 113–14, 179
Glasgow University 210
Gloucester 33
Golding, William 146
Gollins, Annie 34
Gordon, E.V. 123–24, 137
Gordon, George S. 121, 129, 132, 141
Great Hall, Leeds University 121
Great Haywood 91–93, 104
Green, Roger Lancelyn 156, 216
Greeves, Arthur 153, 157, 197
Griffiths, Elaine 157–58
Grimm, Jacob 22, 130
Grove, Jennie 34, 35, 69–70, 75, 86, 91, 108, 111–14, 116, 122–23
Gueroult, Denys 221
Harrogate, Yorkshire 108
Havard, Dr Robert 172, 193
Hornsea, Yorkshire 108, 111–12
Hotel Miramar, Bournemouth 214
Housman, A.E. 46
Hove, E. Sussex 21, 24
Hull 108, 111–12
Incledon, Mary 29–30, 38, 55, 113
Incledon, May 29, 55
Incledon, Marjorie 29–30, 38, 55
Incledon, Walter 29, 55
The Inklings 152, 167, 170 ff., 176, 180–81, 183 ff., 211, 215

Interlaken, Switzerland   52
Ireland   144, 213
Jackson, Peter   157, 213, 215
Jessop, "Aunt" and "Uncle"   64, 68, 69, 112
Johnson, Samuel   88
Kalevala   45, 80, 110
King Edward's School Chronicle   44, 46, 48
Kipling, Rudyard   90
Lakeside Road, Bournemouth   215
Lambourn, Berkshire   61
3rd Lancashire Fusiliers   103, 108
11th Lancashire Fusiliers   94–95, 103–104
19th Lancashire Fusiliers   76, 85, 87
Larkin, Philip   136
Lauterbrunnen, Switzerland   52
Lawlor, John   165–67
Led Zeppelin   215
Leeds University   120, 121, 123, 129
Lewis, C.S.   31, 40, 49, 125, 141–42, 144–45, 147, 149, 150–54, 157, 159, 167 ff., 181 ff., 197–98, 210, 216, 217
Lewis, Warren Hamilton   170, 172, 181, 193, 202–203, 210
Lichfield, Staffordshire   87–88, 90, 92
Llanbedrog, Wales   122
Lyme Regis, Dorset   31, 137, 140
Mabbott, John   143
The Mabinogion   46
MacDonald, George   114, 120, 157
Malvern, Worcestershire   202, 203, 232
The Marvellous Land of Snergs   156
Mascall, E.L.   186
Mathew, Gervase   193
Morgan, Father Francis   19 ff., 55–56, 63, 68, 87, 112, 140

Morris, William   80–81, 120, 157
Morris, William (Lord Nuffield)   58, 195
Neave, Jane (Aunt)   21, 24, 38, 51, 76–77, 129
Newman, Cardinal Henry   18, 20, 25, 26, 123
Norman Conquest   28, 49, 67, 70
Norman, Philip   211
Otley, Yorkshire   92
Oxford Poetry 1915   88
Oxford   57–58
   Addison's Walk   167
   Alfred Street   119–120, 122
   Balliol College, Oxford   215
   Blackwell's Bookshop   57, 88, 195
   Bodleian Library   10, 32, 124, 195
   Broad Street   26, 31, 57, 117, 195
   Corpus Christi College   67
   The Eagle and Child   171, 185, 189, 211
   Eastgate Hotel   152
   Examination Schools   57, 68, 182
   Exeter College   56–58, 65, 67, 79, 81, 119, 151
   Headington   170, 196, 211
   Holywell Street   195, 196
   The Kings Arms   195
   Longwall Street   195
   Magdalen College   141, 152, 166–67, 170, 184, 189
   Manor Road   194–95, 199
   Merton College   132, 141, 151, 170, 189, 194, 211
   Merton Street   218
   Northmoor Road   136, 138, 140, 152, 181–82, 195
   Old Ashmolean   117
   Pembroke College   137, 170, 182, 189
   Sandfield Road   196, 217
   St Aloysius's Church   137
   SS Gregory and Augustine Church   137

St John Street 80, 116

Taylorian Institute 57, 80

Turl Street 57

Oxford English Dictionary 78, 115–17

Paris 70, 71

Payton, Ralph Stuart "The Baby" 47–48, 61, 84, 99

Payton, Wilfred Hugh 47, 61, 84

Phoenix Farm, Gedling 76–78, 129

Plotz, Dick 214

Poetic Edda 111, 151–52

Reynolds, R.W. 49–50, 57, 114

The Ring of Words 116

Rome 179

Roos, Yorkshire 109, 113

Rowling, J.K. 118

Rugeley Camp 113

Sayer, George 202–203

Sayers, Dorothy L. 88

Scout movement 27

The Screwtape Letters 187

Sheaf, Mabel 196

Sheridan, R.B. 43, 46–47, 134

Shippey, T.A. 45–46, 129–130

Shugborough Hall, Staffordshire 92

Sidmouth, Devon 137

Sir Gawain and the Green Knight 67, 123, 152, 210

Sisam, Kenneth 119, 120, 123, 130, 131

Smith, G.B. 44, 46–47, 61, 67, 76, 80, 82–85, 87–91, 93, 97–98, 101, 114

Smith, Mrs Ruth Annie 47, 104, 158

St Andrews University 51, 169, 175–76

St Mark's Terrace, Leeds 123

St Mary Immaculate Church, Warwick 70, 86

Steiner, George 78

Steiner, Rudolf 170

Stewart, J.I.M. 132, 135, 140

Stonyhurst College 70–71, 113, 179–180, 213

Suffield, Auntie Bea (Beatrice) 25, 32

Sumner, Sydney 99, 100

Swann, Donald 171, 218

Switzerland 51–53

T.C.B.S. 42–48, 61, 74, 81–84, 88, 90, 94–102, 104, 144, 149, 152, 167

Tea Club *see T.C.B.S.*

Thirtle Bridge Camp, Yorkshire 108, 111, 112

Three Cups Hotel, Lyme Regis 31

The Tolkien Family Album 51

Tolkien, Christopher 129, 166, 179–180, 193, 220

Tolkien, Edith (nee Bratt) 32–37, 38, 55–56, 60, 62–64, 68–70, 74–75, 86–87, 91–92, 93, 108–111, 122, 125, 129, 137 ff., 163–64, 181, 182, 196–97, 213–15, 218–19

Tolkien, Hilary 13, 16, 19, 21, 26, 40, 51, 75–76, 104, 128

Tolkien, John 112, 125, 140, 156, 179, 195

Tolkien, John Ronald Reuel, *see Writings of J.R.R. Tolkien*

Tolkien, Lawrence 25

Tolkien, Mabel (nee Suffield) 11–23, 24, 67

Tolkien, Michael 112, 122, 123, 126–27, 128, 140, 156, 163, 179, 195, 199

Tolkien, Priscilla 138, 179, 182, 196, 213

Tolkien, Christopher 9, 110, 157, 220

Tracey, Gerard 221

Trought, Vincent 48, 72, 96

University of Liège 212
Unwin, Raynor 158, 200–201
Unwin, Sir Stanley 158–59, 201
Venice 214
Viking Club 124
W.P. Ker Memorial Lecture 210
Wain, John 190
Waldman, Milton 200–201
Wandsworth, London 82
Warrillow, Alfred Frederick 33, 56, 222
Warwick 69–70, 74–75, 86–87, 89
Wayland's Smithy 163
Whitby, Yorkshire 126
Williams, Charles 81, 135, 180, 181, 183–87, 189, 190, 197
Wilson, A.N. 9, 149
Wilson, F.P. 194
Wiseman, Christopher 41–42, 44, 47, 50, 61, 74, 82–83, 88, 90, 94, 108, 114, 129, 144–45, 216
Withernsea, Yorkshire 108–109
Worminghall, Buckinghamshire 164
Wrenn, Agnes 166, 196
Wrenn, Charles L. 166–67, 172
Wright, Joseph 45, 46, 59, 120
Writings of J.R.R. Tolkien:
    "The Adventures of Tom Bombadil" 163
    The tale of Beren and Lúthien 106, 109, 111, 149–151, 219
    "Bimble Bay" 126, 128
    The Book of Lost Tales 104, 106, 107, 110, 111, 113, 119
    "Errantry" 171
    Farmer Giles of Ham 164, 216
    The Father Christmas Letters 122
    "The Fall of Gondolin" 104 ff., 119
    "Goblin Feet" 88
    The History of Middle-earth 220

The Hobbit 155–161
"Imram" 210
"Kortirion Among the Trees" 89
Leaf by Niggle 187, 188, 189, 217
The Lord of the Rings 204–209
The Lost Road 159, 180, 210
The Monsters and the Critics 173
Mr Bliss 162
Mythopoeia 167, 168
The Notion Club Papers 14, 23
"On Fairy Stories" 169, 173, 216
Roverandom 126, 127
"A Secret Vice" 151
The Silmarillion (and "The Silmarillion") 79, 107–108, 130, 149–150, 159, 200–201, 209, 220
Smith of Wootton Major 216
Unfinished Tales 106, 220
"Wood-sunshine" 42, 50
Wyke-Smith, E.A. 156
Yeats, W.B. 46